W9-BIE-221

DK Pocket Genius

SPORTS

FACTS AT YOUR FINGERTIPS

Penguin
Random
House

Senior Editor Rupa Rao
Senior Art Editor Vikas Chauhan
Project Art Editor Mansi Agrawal
Project Editor Kathakali Banerjee
Editors Bharti Bedi, Priyanka Kharbanda
US Editor Christopher Stolle **US Executive Editor** Lori Cates Hand
Picture Research Co-ordinator Sumita Khatwani
Assistant Picture Research Researcher Vagisha Pushp
Picture Research Manager Taiyaba Khatoon
Managing Editor Kingshuk Ghoshal
Managing Art Editor Govind Mittal
Senior DTP Designer Jagtar Singh
DTP Designers Jaypal Singh Chauhan, Rakesh Kumar
Pre-production Manager Balwant Singh
Production Manager Pankaj Sharma
Production Editor Gillian Reid
Production Controller Sian Cheung
Jacket Designer Juhi Sheth
DK India Editorial Head Glenda Fernandes
Jacket Design Head Malavika Talukder
Jacket Design Development Manager Sophia MTT
Publisher Andrew Macintyre
Associate Publishing Director Liz Wheeler
Art Director Karen Self
Publishing Director Jonathan Metcalf

Author Clive Gifford
Consultants Brian Burnsed, Steven Conway,
Megan Fernandez, John Schwarb, Christopher Stolle

This title was created with support from the DK Diversity,
Equity, & Inclusion team. Thanks to the Product and
Content Working Group for their input and guidance.

First American Edition, 2021
Published in the United States by DK Publishing
1745 Broadway, 20th Floor, New York, NY 10019

Copyright © 2021 Dorling Kindersley Limited
DK, a Division of Penguin Random House LLC
22 23 24 25 10 9 8 7 6 5 4 3 2
002–322653–Dec/2021

A catalog record for this book
is available from the Library of Congress.
ISBN 978-0-7440-3961-0

DK books are available at special discounts when purchased in bulk
for sales promotions, premiums, fund-raising, or educational use.
For details, contact: DK Publishing Special Markets,
1745 Broadway, 20th Floor, New York, NY 10019
SpecialSales@dk.com

Printed and bound in China

For the curious

www.dk.com

MIX
Paper from
responsible sources
FSC™ C018179

This book was made with Forest
Stewardship Council™ certified
paper – one small step in DK's
commitment to a sustainable
future. For more information go to
www.dk.com/our-green-pledge

There are many wonderful sports out there. This book
doesn't cover all of them but does feature some of the
popular ones from around the world.

The sports in this book should be played by children
under appropriate parental supervision and after
taking necessary safety precautions.

Given next to the entry for each sport is information
about some of the following: where and how the sport
is contested and won; how long it lasts; what some of
its major events are; whether it is played by individuals
(solo), pairs (duo), or teams; and what the players use
or wear (gear) while playing it.

CONTENTS

What is a sport?

Sports are activities in which people use physical effort and skill to compete against others. Some sports pit two individuals head-to-head, while others are team contests. People play sports for fun, exercise, the challenge, or the thrill of competition.

Differing demands

Each sport requires something different. Some call for great strength, explosive power, or lightning-fast reactions. Others need strategy and accuracy. But all players need to practice the skills and techniques that will give them the winning edge.

A weightlifter needs strong muscles to lift heavy weights.

An archer needs calm concentration, steady arms, and a good aim.

Archery

Weightlifting

Games

Competitive activities that involve skill, knowledge, or chance but rarely any physical activity are called games. Examples include card games, checkers, and chess, which some consider a sport because of the serious nature of its contests.

A panel of judges watches the competitors perform.

eSports

Competitive video gaming draws large crowds of live and internet viewers. In such eSports, individual gamers or teams compete within one computer game.

Play by the rules

All competitive sports have rules. Many of them have officials, such as basketball referees, who monitor play and ensure the rules are followed. In some sports, such as diving or gymnastics, a panel of judges decides the score of each competitor.

Adapted for all

The adrenaline rush of playing a sport can be enjoyed by people of all ages and abilities. Some sports, such as flag rugby, have been adapted for younger children by making it safer for them to play. Other sports, such as the 200 m sprint, have been adapted to allow athletes with disabilities to compete. As seen here, visually impaired British athlete Libby Clegg (left) competes in a race with the assistance of a nondisabled guide (right).

Ancient sports

No one knows precisely when sports first began. But evidence found in cave paintings and other rock art make it clear that people have been taking part in competitions of speed, strength, and skill for thousands of years. The depictions show players competing in many sports, including wrestling, sprinting, swimming, and archery.

Ancient Olympics

The Olympics are the world's biggest sporting competition. The first Olympics were held in 776 BCE and featured just one race. Over time, more events, including boxing, wrestling, the long jump, and throwing a discus, were added.

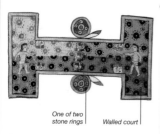

One of two stone rings | Walled court

Early ball game

A 16th century Aztec manuscript shows an ancient Mesoamerican ball game being played by at least two players. Estimated to have been first played over 3,000 years ago, in Mexico and Central America, the sport featured players trying to propel a solid ball made of natural rubber through one of two stone rings on a walled court.

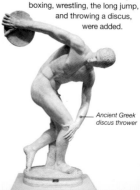

Ancient Greek discus thrower

Cuju

A forerunner of football, cuju was first played in ancient China more than 2,000 years ago. Without using their hands, cuju players score goals by kicking a ball between bamboo poles or into a hole.

Military training

During training, ancient armies would competitively practice their skills—from spear throwing to wrestling. Some sports arose out of these training competitions, including chariot racing, which drew huge crowds in ancient Rome.

Lacrosse

A stick and ball game played by the Algonquian tribe and other indigenous Americans was named lacrosse by French settlers in the 1630s. A modified version of the sport is still played today.

Playing sports

Millions of people enjoy playing sports, which fascinate us as children and inspire passion and pride as we grow up. Most sports have dedicated regional, national, or world championship competitions, which offer players or teams a chance to compete against each other for victory and glory.

The Italian men's football team after winning UEFA Euro 2020

Organized sports

Sports need to be organized for large competitions. Most sports are governed by national associations. Many of these answer to continental federations, such as UEFA for football in Europe, and to global organizations, such as FINA for swimming. These bodies arrange rules and major international competitions.

Clubs and leagues

Many global sporting superstars started out—like these children (right)—at their local sports club. Such organizations offer training and a chance to compete against others. A sports league, such as the National Hockey League (NHL), often contains a set of teams that all play each other during a season.

Sports in schools and colleges

Sports offer school students fun experiences, challenges, ways of gaining physical fitness, and chances to build friendships. As they progress, a young athlete may seek to go further. In some countries, sports scholarships to colleges offer a vital springboard to establishing a career in a sport.

A US college volleyball game

Olympics

After being banned by the Romans in 400 CE, the Olympics were revived in 1896. The Summer Olympics are held every four years in the summer months (but were postponed in 2020 because of the COVID-19 pandemic). The Winter Olympics are a separate version of the Games for winter sports. Winners at the Olympic Games are given a gold medal, the second-placed players win silver, and those who place third win bronze.

Silver

Bronze

Gold

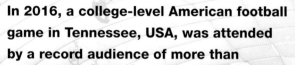

In 2016, a college-level American football game in Tennessee, USA, was attended by a record audience of more than

156,000 people

SPLENDID STADIUM
The Metrodome, in Minneapolis, USA, is where a crowd of more than 62,000 American football fans gathered to watch the Minnesota Vikings defeat the Atlanta Falcons in 2007. The thousands of fans at large stadiums not only cheer their teams but also unite in the spirit of the sport.

Sports for all

Athletes with disabilities—physical, intellectual, or sensory conditions that limit a person's activities—play many sports. At an international level, the Paralympics and the Special Olympics offer opportunities for many disabled athletes to compete in organized sports.

French long jumper
Marie-Amélie Le Fur

Light carbon fiber blade enables high speeds.

Adaptive sports

The equipment and rules for some sports have been modified so disabled players can play and experience them. Adaptive sports include wheelchair tennis (below) and para-cycling.

Dutch player
Aniek van Koot

Paralympics

Athletes with a wide range of disabilities compete in the Paralympics (or Parallel Olympics), which take place shortly after each Olympic Games. Participants, known as Paralympians, take part in hundreds of sporting events.

New sports

To offer more opportunities for talented disabled players to take up playing a sport, whole new sports have been developed for the Paralympics. These include goalball (above), in which visually impaired athletes play with a ball that has bells embedded in it to make a sound as it moves.

Special Olympics

Athletes with intellectual disabilities—conditions that limit a person's learning, thinking, or adaptive skills—can compete in the Special Olympics, held every four years, or in related annual competitions. These focus on personal achievements and feature events in more than 30 sports, including soccer (right).

Track and field & Gymnastics

A burning desire to be the best marks out elite athletes and gymnasts. Most events in these sports pit a lone sportsperson up against many other competitors over a number of qualifying rounds before the final competition. So talent and dedication to training must also come with a fierce will to win.

SPECTACULAR VAULT
German gymnast Matthias Fahrig springs off a vault table in a strong routine at a European Championship event in 2013.

FOCUS ON...
TRIATHLONS
In an endurance event, athletes have to compete in multiple sports in sequence. A triathlon combines the sports of swimming, cycling, and racing in the same event.

▲ The competition begins with an open water swim over a course that can be up to 2.4 miles (3.9 km) long.

◀ The athletes cycle next and might cover up to 112 miles (180.2 km).

◀ The final stage is a grueling run, or a marathon, to the finish line, covering a distance up to 26 miles (42.2 km).

Track and Field

Tests of speed and stamina, these events include events held on tracks, such as walking and running races, and those played on fields, such as jumping and throwing events.

Sprints

The fastest track races are sprints. These short-distance running events are held over 60 m, 100 m, 200 m, and 400 m, with only the 60 m sprints happening indoors. Each race requires explosive muscle power at the start as well as excellent technique and rhythm to pump arms and legs for maintaining a high speed throughout the race. For each type of sprint, the winner is the athlete who is first to cross the finish line with their chest.

TYPE Track event, solo

GEAR Running spikes, close-fitted clothes

HELD ON Indoor and outdoor tracks

British athlete Richard Whitehead runs in a 200 m para-athletics event during the 2018 Müller Anniversary Games in the UK.

Hurdles

Held over 110 m and 400 m for men and over 100 m and 400 m for women, hurdle races feature 10 barriers that the athletes have to go over as they run to the finish line.

TYPE	Track event, solo
GEAR	Running spikes
HELD ON	Indoor and outdoor tracks

Relays

In this team event, each of the four athletes on a team run a part (leg) of the race, usually 100 m or 400 m, passing a stick called a baton to the next runner as smoothly and quickly as possible.

TYPE	Track event, team
GEAR	Running spikes, 12 in (30 cm) long baton
HELD ON	Indoor and outdoor tracks

Long-distance races

Athletes are tested to the limits of their endurance in these races, which can vary from an 800 m race to a 26.2 mile (42.2 km) long marathon. In most events, athletes run multiple laps of the track, although some are held on cross-country or street circuits.

TYPE	Track event, solo
GEAR	Running spikes or road shoes
HELD ON	Outdoor tracks, city streets, cross-country courses

A 100 m hurdler can clear all 10 barriers in their lane in just

12.5 seconds

FLOWING OVER HURDLES

Athletes compete in a high hurdles event at the 2018 Women's 100 m World Athletics Under 20 Championship in Finland. Sprint hurdle events use higher barriers than the longer-distance hurdle races. Competing in high hurdle races requires good timing and flexibility as the runners clear the barriers with barely any change in pace or their stride pattern.

Starts and finishes

All track races have a start and finish, with competitors aiming to cross the finishing line in the quickest time. Most races are held on outdoor oval tracks divided into running lanes. Depending on the event, athletes might have to stay in their lane throughout.

Starting blocks
Angled blocks provide a platform for a sprinter's feet to push hard against at the start of a race. The athlete drives forward and upward out of the blocks as they take their first racing strides.

Staggered starts
In 200 m, 400 m, and 800 m events and in 4x100 m relay races, athletes start from different positions in their own lanes so they all cover the same distance, allowing for the track bend.

Standing start
Used for longer-distance events, standing starts involve runners lined up behind a single line, leaning forward with their weight on the ball of their front foot and the toes of their back foot. They are poised, ready to run on the starter's signal.

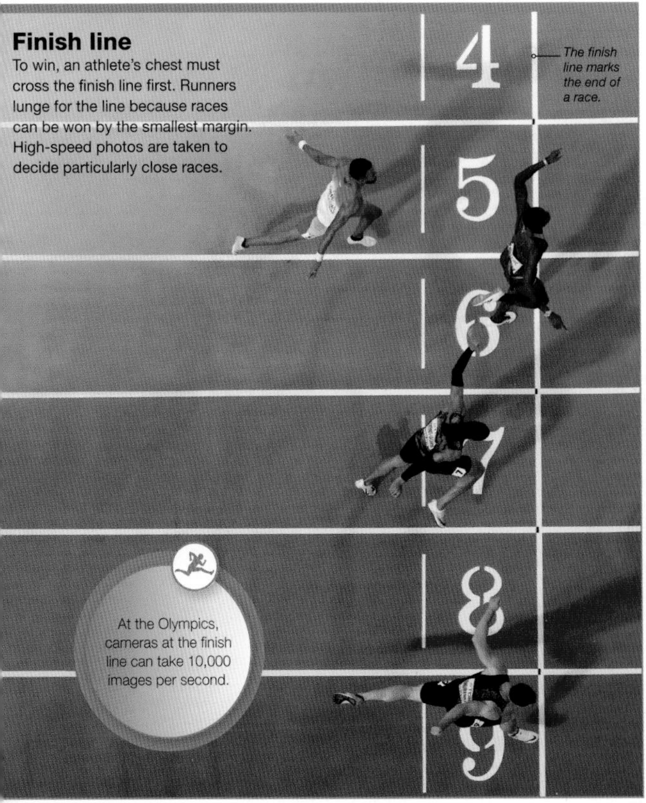

Finish line

To win, an athlete's chest must cross the finish line first. Runners lunge for the line because races can be won by the smallest margin. High-speed photos are taken to decide particularly close races.

The finish line marks the end of a race.

4

5

6

7

8

9

At the Olympics, cameras at the finish line can take 10,000 images per second.

Shot put

In this throwing event, a powerful body and arm drive push a heavy metal ball (the shot) up and away as far as possible. A shot-putter can improve their grip on the shot by rubbing chalk into their hands.

TYPE Field event, solo

GEAR Shot

HELD ON Throwing circle, 7 ft (2.1 m) in diameter

In 1990, US athlete Randy Barnes set a men's world record by putting the shot 75.8 ft (23.12 m).

Ukrainian athlete Ihor Mussijenko puts a shot at the 2020 Ukrainian Athletics Indoor Championships.

Discus

A thrower spins around in a circle before their arm whips forward to release the discus from a sidearm position. The distance of the throw is measured from the front of the throwing circle to the point where the discus first lands.

TYPE Field event, solo

GEAR Discus (disc made of rubber and metal or wood)

HELD ON Throwing circle, 8 ft (2.5 m) in diameter

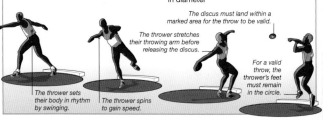

The discus must land within a marked area for the throw to be valid.

The thrower stretches their throwing arm before releasing the discus.

For a valid throw, the thrower's feet must remain in the circle.

The thrower sets their body in rhythm by swinging.

The thrower spins to gain speed.

Hammer

Standing within the throwing circle, the athlete swings the hammer (a heavy metal ball on a cable) to throw it as far as possible. They spin themselves to build speed before finally timing the hammer's release.

TYPE Field event, solo

GEAR Hammer

HELD ON Throwing circle, 7 ft (2.1 m) in diameter

Javelin

After sprinting down to the throwing line, athletes hurl their spear-like javelin. It must land tip first for the throw to be valid. Athletes receive three or six attempts depending on the competition.

TYPE Field event, solo

GEAR Javelin

HELD ON Runway, at least 120 ft (36.5 m) long

Long jump

In this jumping event, athletes try to jump farther than anyone else. After a powerful sprint, they leap from the take-off board and stretch their bodies to make the jump last longer. Then they push their legs forward to land in a sandpit. Athletes will usually have three or six chances to jump.

TYPE	Field event, solo
GEAR	Jumping spikes
HELD ON	Runway and landing pit, 33 ft (10 m) long

US athlete Christian Taylor jumps at the 2012 British Grand Prix.

Triple jump

Combining a hop and a step with a jump, the triple jump event sees an athlete leap off one foot, which they must land on before hopping forward on it. Then they take as long a bounding step as possible with the other foot and jump into a sandpit. Athletes are judged on greatest overall distance covered.

The athlete makes the hop without touching the take-off line.

The athlete takes one long step in midair.

The athlete prepares to launch into a jump from the foot on which they landed.

| Take off | Hop | | Step |

High jump

An athlete must jump higher than their competitors to win this event. They get multiple attempts at jumping over a bar at a set height after an initial sprint. The athlete jumps off one foot and arches backward over the bar to clear it.

TYPE Field event, solo

GEAR High jump shoes with spikes in the heels

HELD ON Jumping area, 16.5 ft (5 m) long, with runway, crossbar, and crash mat

The bar falls easily if touched by a jumper and is raised with each successful jump.

TYPE Field event, solo

GEAR Jumping spikes

HELD ON Runway and landing pit, 29.5 ft (9 m) long

The athlete uses one of many techniques to jump.

The athlete lands feetfirst in the sand, throwing their weight forward.

Jump

Pole vault

A vaulter sprints with a flexible pole and then plants it in the ground, making it bend almost double under their weight. As the pole straightens, it propels the vaulter, now upside down, over a high bar.

TYPE Field event, solo

GEAR Long flexible pole

HELD ON Vaulting area, 16.5 ft (5 m) long, with runway, crossbar, and landing mat

Gymnastics

This group of sports includes events in which gymnasts compete on different apparatus to score the highest points. A panel of judges marks their performance. Gymnastics has three main sections: rhythmic gymnastics, artistic gymnastics, and trampoline.

Rhythmic gymnastics

Gymnasts perform graceful ballet routines in time to music while using equipment—ball, hoop, ribbon, club, or rope—without a pause.

TYPE	Solo or team (up to five gymnasts)
GEAR	Apparatus
HELD ON	Performance area, 43 ft (13 m) on each side

The gymnast moves apparatus, such as a hoop, with their hands and body.

The gymnast must keep their head upright to maintain balance.

FOCUS ON...
APPARATUS

Rhythmic gymnasts work with different pieces of equipment—each demanding a specific skill. Each piece has its own rules.

▲ The 14.1 oz (400 g) rubber ball is rolled, thrown, and balanced.

▲ The wooden or plastic hoop is thrown, spun, or jumped through.

▲ The ribbon is twirled continuously, forming different shapes in the air.

Floor exercises

One of the events under artistic gymnastics, floor exercises mix spectacular acrobatic tumbling with such moves as controlled handstands, jumps, and balances that show poise and flexibility.

TYPE Solo or team (up to four gymnasts)

GEAR Hand chalk for grip

HELD ON Square rubber floor mat, 39 ft (12 m) on each side

German
gymnast
Kim Bui

US artistic gymnast Simone Biles has four gymnastic moves named after her.

Vaults

Vaulters build speed along a runway before leaping off a springboard toward a vault table. Once their hands touch the table, competitors must perform twists or somersaults in flight. Their landing must be balanced and on both feet.

TYPE Solo or team (up to four gymnasts)

GEAR Wrist supports, hand chalk for grip

HELD ON Vault runway, springboard, and vault table, up to 4.4 ft (1.35 m) high

Pommel horse

In this event, male gymnasts perform a continuous routine with their legs swinging around a pommel horse. They can touch the pommel horse with only their hands.

TYPE Solo or team (up to four gymnasts)

GEAR Wrist sweatbands, hand chalk, tights with stirrups

HELD ON Pommel horse, 4 ft (1.15 m) tall

Pommel (handle)

Bar events

An example of artistic gymnastics, bar events are of three types: uneven bars for women and horizontal and parallel bars for men. On uneven and horizontal bars, gymnasts release then re-grip the bars, performing twists or somersaults in between. On parallel bars, gymnasts perform swinging movements and displays of strength.

The gymnast swings between two bars.

Balance beam

Female gymnasts perform eye-catching routines along the length of a wooden beam, displaying balance and strength, and end with a spectacular dismount.

TYPE Solo or team (up to four gymnasts)

GEAR Hand chalk

HELD ON Beam, 16.5 ft (5 m) long

TYPE	Solo or team (up to four gymnasts)
GEAR	Handgrips, hand chalk
HELD ON	Bar apparatus on a raised podium

Nadia Comăneci received the first perfect score on the uneven bars at the 1976 Olympics.

British gymnast Joe Fraser performs on parallel bars.

Each bar is 11.5 ft (3.5 m) long and the two are set 17–20 in (42–52 cm) apart.

Rings

The steel cables, covered with plastic, are strong and flexible.

The gymnast uses their upper body strength to keep the rings as steady as possible.

Strength and balance are useful when competing on the rings. In this event, a pair of rings is suspended above the ground. Male gymnasts swing backward and forward, and they hold a number of set positions before dismounting.

TYPE	Solo or team (up to four gymnasts)
GEAR	Wrist supports, hand chalk
HELD ON	Rings hanging from the ceiling or a freestanding frame

In a 90-second beam routine, a gymnast must make a

360-degree turn

Weightlifting

Like gymnastics, weightlifting occurs indoors under the eye of judges. Lifters get three attempts to lift a barbell at a set weight, and with a successful lift, the weight on the bar is increased. A competitor wins by lifting the heaviest weight.

TYPE Solo

GEAR One-piece outfit that ends above the knee, support belt

HELD IN Weightlifting arena

Different colors indicate different weights.

Aýsoltan Toýçyýewa of Turkmenistan competes at the 2017 Asian Indoor and Martial Arts Games in Ashgabat, Turkmenistan.

Powerlifting

Each lifter must lift a set weight from three different positions—squat, deadlift, and bench press (below)—and they have three attempts at each one. Weights lifted are added up for a final score.

TYPE Solo

GEAR Smooth-soled shoes, wrist wraps

HELD ON Powerlifting platform

Trampolining

Gymnasts bounce on a spring-bound bed called a trampoline to build height before embarking on a routine of acrobatic twists, dives, and somersaults.

TYPE Solo or duo

GEAR Leotards or unitards or vest and pants, trampolining shoes

HELD ON Trampoline, 14 ft (4.3 m) long

Tumbling

Judges score routines in which athletes flip, twist, and somersault while only placing their hands or feet on the ground. Skills displayed include flicks and roundoffs.

TYPE Solo or team

GEAR Close-fitting bodysuit

HELD ON Sprung track, 82 ft (25 m) long

Racewalking

Competitors walk a specific distance during a race. They must keep their leading leg straight and at least one foot must stay in contact with the ground throughout a race.

TYPE Solo or team

GEAR Vest, shorts, racewalking shoes

HELD ON Track, road course

The body is upright for balance.

Small, quick steps help to walk fast.

Team sports

Some of the world's most-watched sports involve two teams of competitors. While every player might have abilities and techniques they have mastered, they will each have a role on their team, support their teammates, and work together toward a common goal: winning as one team.

FLYING HIGH
Players on a team might band together to help one teammate. In this rugby union game, the team lifts their forward so he can secure the ball at a lineout.

Team sports

In a team sport, different players on the team use their skills to coordinate with each other when defending, attacking, and scoring goals or points to win. Such team sports as football and basketball are some of the most popular sports in the world.

FOCUS ON...
REFEREE SIGNALS

A team of officials runs a game, led by a referee, who uses hand signals to communicate decisions.

▲ The offense has advanced enough to earn a first down.

▲ A player has illegally held back an opponent during play.

▲ A player has interfered with an opponent during a passing play.

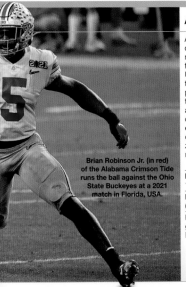

Brian Robinson Jr. (in red) of the Alabama Crimson Tide runs the ball against the Ohio State Buckeyes at a 2021 match in Florida, USA.

American football

An epic battle of strategy, big collisions, and spectacular plays makes for a game of American football, known as just football in the US. Each team tries to advance up the field using passing and running plays, aiming to move the ball into their opponent's end zone to score a touchdown worth six points. Points can also be scored in other ways—even by a defensive team tackling opponent players in their own end zone. The ultimate aim is to score more points than the other team.

PLAYERS Two teams of 11 players each

DURATION 60 minutes (four 15-minute quarters)

PLAYED ON Field (called gridiron), 120 yd (109.75 m) long and 53 yd (48.8 m) wide

The offense

In American football, the offense is the team that has the ball and advances toward the end zone of the opposing team, the defense. The offense gets four chances, or downs, to move the ball 10 yd (9 m). If it fails or loses the ball during play, then the teams switch roles.

Different plays

The leader of the offense is the quarterback, who communicates the next play to their teammates. This might be a running play, such as a blast where a player called the running back drives through the defensive line, or a passing play with a throw to a receiver upfield.

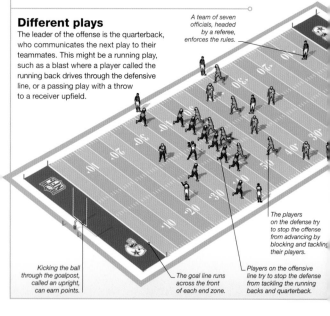

A team of seven officials, headed by a referee, enforces the rules.

The players on the defense try to stop the offense from advancing by blocking and tackling their players.

Kicking the ball through the goalpost, called an upright, can earn points.

The goal line runs across the front of each end zone.

Players on the offensive line try to stop the defense from tackling the running backs and quarterback.

Playbook

Coaches select the plays for a team from a large selection of set moves in their playbook that have been practiced in training. On the field, the quarterback (right) usually orchestrates the play. In pauses between downs, players regroup in order to discuss the next play.

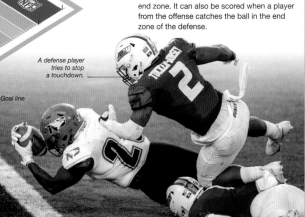

Each end zone is 10 yd (9 m) deep.

Touchdown

A touchdown is scored when a player from the offense runs with the ball over the goal line that marks the front of the opposition's end zone. It can also be scored when a player from the offense catches the ball in the end zone of the defense.

A defense player tries to stop a touchdown.

Goal line

FOCUS ON...
TOP
SCORERS

Goals win games, so the players who score most often are highly prized members of their club or national team.

◄ Lionel Messi of Argentina had scored 748 goals for his national team and his clubs by early 2021.

◄ Brazilian legend Pelé scored 1,279 goals for his country and clubs during his 20-year career.

◄ By early 2021, Portuguese star Cristiano Ronaldo had scored a total of 783 goals for his country and clubs.

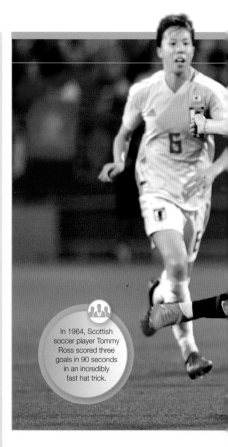

In 1964, Scottish soccer player Tommy Ross scored three goals in 90 seconds in an incredibly fast hat trick.

Soccer

Speed and skill combine in soccer, the world's most popular team sport. Players defend their 8 yd (7.32 m) wide goal while attempting to kick or head the ball into their opponent's goal. In a game, players pass, head, shoot, and control the ball with their head, body, or feet. Only the goalkeeper on each team can touch the ball with their hands. Fans of the sport follow many competitions between national teams and those between clubs.

PLAYERS Two teams of 11 players each

DURATION 90 minutes (two 45-minute halves)

PLAYED ON Grass or artificial pitch, 100–130 yd (90–120 m) long and 50–100 yd (45–90 m) wide

US soccer player Megan Rapinoe kicks the ball in a match against Japan at the 2020 SheBelieves Cup in Texas, USA.

Rugby union

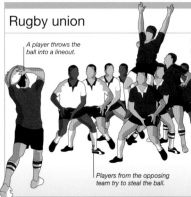

A player throws the ball into a lineout.

Players from the opposing team try to steal the ball.

In this sport of throws, kicks, and passes, two teams strive to score points, or tries, by touching the ball down in their opponent's in-goal area. The ball can be run with or kicked forward, but passes must travel sideway or backward.

PLAYERS Two teams of 15 players each

DURATION 80 minutes (two 40-minute halves)

PLAYED ON Pitch, up to 400 ft (122 m) long and 230 ft (70 m) wide

Rugby league

Teams have fewer players in this version of rugby. In a league game, the attacking team need only be tackled six times before the possession of the ball passes to the defending team. This is unlike a union game, which allows unlimited tackles.

PLAYERS Two teams of 13 players each

DURATION 80 minutes (two 40-minute halves)

PLAYED ON Pitch, up to 400 ft (122 m) long and 223 ft (68 m) wide

Australian football

Two teams compete to control an oval ball in this fast-paced sport. Players tackle their opponents to prevent them from scoring points, which is done by kicking the ball into the opposing team's goal area—a set of four vertical poles. This sport is known as "Aussie Rules" in Australia.

PLAYERS Two teams of 18 players each

DURATION 80 minutes (four 20-minute quarters)

PLAYED ON Oval field, up to 607 ft (185 m) long and 508.5 ft (155 m) wide

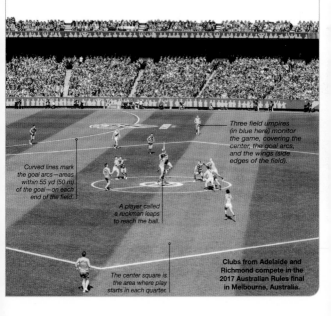

Three field umpires (in blue here) monitor the game, covering the center, the goal arcs, and the wings (side edges of the field).

Curved lines mark the goal arcs—areas within 55 yd (50 m) of the goal—on each end of the field.

A player called a ruckman leaps to reach the ball.

The center square is the area where play starts in each quarter.

Clubs from Adelaide and Richmond compete in the 2017 Australian Rules final in Melbourne, Australia.

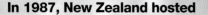

In 1987, New Zealand hosted

16 countries

at the first Rugby World Cup

THE MIGHTY ALL BLACKS
New Zealand forward Brodie Retallick is tackled short of the try line in a 2018 Rugby Championship match against Australia, which was won by Retallick's team: the New Zealand All Blacks. They are the country's men's national rugby union team, and by 2020, they had won this championship 16 times.

Cricket

Two teams take turns to bat, looking to strike the ball and score as many runs (points) as possible. While one team bats, the other—called the fielding team—tries to bowl them out and keep the batters from scoring runs.

PLAYERS Two teams of 11 players each

DURATION 20 or 50 overs of six balls per team, or at least 90 overs of six balls per day (over 3–5 days)

PLAYED ON Flat field with a central rectangular pitch, 22 yd (20.1 m) long and 10 ft (3 m) wide

Test match between India and England in Birmingham, UK

Fielders try to catch the ball before it touches the ground to get the batter out.

Softball

A popular sport, softball developed from baseball, but it is played with a bigger ball that is always thrown underarm toward the batter. Players score runs by running around the four bases—just like in baseball.

PLAYERS Two teams of nine players each

DURATION Seven innings for each team to bat and field

PLAYED ON Softball field with a diamond-shaped square infield, 60 ft (18.29 m) on each side

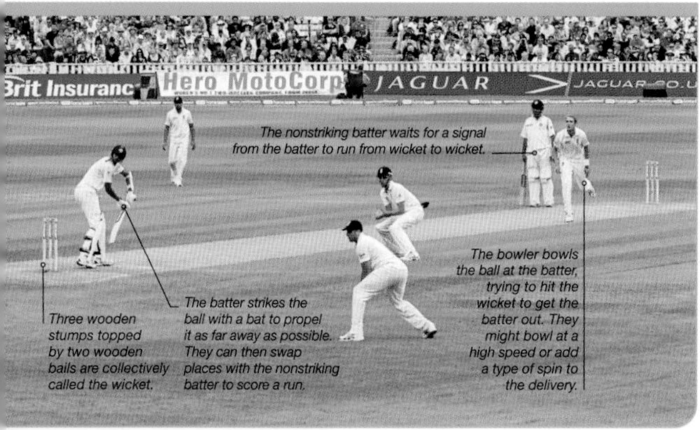

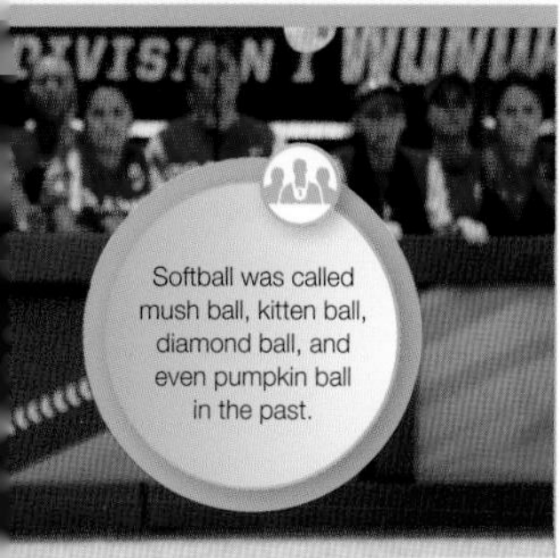

Softball was called mush ball, kitten ball, diamond ball, and even pumpkin ball in the past.

US softball player Jocelyn Alo plays in the 2021 Women's Softball Championship in Oklahoma, USA.

Handball

Over the course of an action-packed hour, players on two teams use their hands to pass a ball and score goals past the opposing team's goalkeeper.

PLAYERS Two teams of seven players each

DURATION 60 minutes

PLAYED ON Rectangular court, 131 ft (40 m) long and 65.6 ft (20 m) wide

FOCUS ON...
HOME RUNS

A home run is when a player hits the ball over the outfield fence or can touch all four bases before being tagged out. Here are some great home run hitters.

◀ Henry "Hank" Aaron struck 755 home runs during his career.

◀ Babe Ruth hit 714 home runs—a mark that stood for almost 40 years.

◀ Ken Griffey Jr. smacked 630 home runs in his 22-year career.

Baseball

Two teams take turns, known as innings, batting and pitching. Standing at a base (position) called home plate, a batter tries to hit a ball thrown by the other team's pitcher. A batter's goal is to run to at least first base, move other runners around the bases, or hit home runs —or a combination of these—before their team makes three outs. The opposing team tries to prevent the batting team from scoring by using good pitching and fielding.

PLAYERS	Two teams of nine players each
DURATION	Nine innings of up to 20 minutes
PLAYED ON	Baseball field

Baseball games have been played for more than 140 years at Canada's Labatt Park, which has the world's oldest baseball field.

US baseball player Juan Soto of the Washington Nationals hits a solo home run during the fourth inning in Game One of the 2019 World Series in Texas, USA.

Baseball field

The power of a pitcher is as important as the sharp reflexes of a batter in baseball, which is played on a field split into outfield and infield areas. The playing area on the field is between the two foul lines.

When a ball travels over one of the two foul lines, it goes out of play and the batter is not allowed to run.

The field

Positions called the four bases (first, second, and third base, and home plate) form a diamond shape in the infield. Most of the action takes place in and around the diamond. The area outside the infield grass line is the outfield, which is bordered by the outfield fence. Patrolling the field are seven fielders: three outfielders and four infielders.

An outfielder tries to catch hit balls and they also return base hits to one of the three infielders.

Key equipment

The 3 in (7.5 cm) wide ball is made of cork or rubber and sealed in a leather casing. Bats are wooden or metal and no longer than 42 in (106.7 cm). Leather gloves are padded for protection.

Ball

Gloves

Bat

The outfield fence marks the far edge of the playing area.

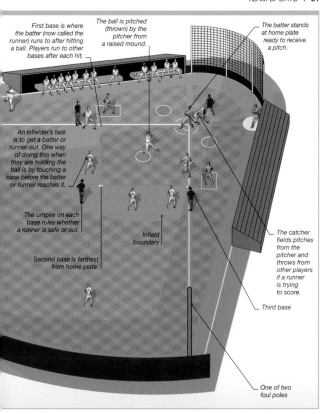

First base is where the batter (now called the runner) runs to after hitting a ball. Players run to other bases after each hit.

The ball is pitched (thrown) by the pitcher from a raised mound.

The batter stands at home plate ready to receive a pitch.

An infielder's task is to get a batter or runner out. One way of doing this when they are holding the ball is by touching a base before the batter or runner reaches it.

The umpire on each base rules whether a runner is safe or out.

Infield boundary

Second base is farthest from home plate.

The catcher fields pitches from the pitcher and throws from other players if a runner is trying to score.

Third base

One of two foul poles

FOCUS ON...
PASSES

A player can move the ball around by passing it to a teammate. They can pass the ball in different ways.

▲ For a bounce pass, a player bounces the ball off the floor and into their teammate's hands.

▲ For an overhead pass, a player throws the ball with arms extending up above their head.

▲ For a chest pass, a player throws the ball parallel to the floor at chest height.

Basketball

Two teams pass and dribble a ball around a court in this sport, aiming to score more points than the other by shooting the ball through their opponent's hooped basket. This sport is very popular in the US, where college games attract as much attention as professional games, which are run by the National Basketball Association (NBA) for men and the Women's National Basketball Association (WNBA) for women.

PLAYERS Two teams of five players each

DURATION
48 minutes

PLAYED ON
Rectangular court, up to 94 ft (28.6 m) long and 50 ft (15.2 m) wide

Legendary US player Michael Jordan played 1,072 NBA games, averaging 30.1 points per game.

Los Angeles Lakers player Kobe Bryant goes in for a slam dunk during a 2001 NBA game in California, USA.

The basket, which has a hoop 18 in (45 cm) in diameter, hangs 10 ft (3.05 m) above the court.

A basket scored from outside this line is worth three points, while one scored from inside it is worth two points.

Hardwood court

Playing basketball

A fast-moving sport, basketball relies on teamwork and individual brilliance. Players must constantly move around the court, trying to pass or shoot the ball or block the shots of the opposing team.

Movement and stance

Players stay light and springy on their feet, ready to move in any direction. As seen here, they might adopt the triple threat stance, from which they can pass, shoot, or dribble the ball.

Ball held close to the hip

Foot held slightly forward

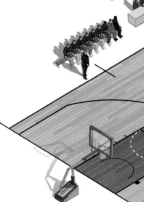

Starting the game

A player from each team stands near the midcourt line as a referee throws the ball into the air to start a game. They try to grab the ball or tip it to a teammate. The point guard of the attacking team then organizes a play, passing or shooting themselves.

Any one of the seven substitutes can switch positions with an on-court player.

The sideline marks the court on each side.

The baseline marks the end of the court.

The backboard is made of reinforced plastic, glass, or fiberglass and is used to deflect the ball into the basket.

From this free throw line, a player can take an unopposed shot worth one point if successful.

The midcourt line separates the court into two halves.

The player drives the ball down and ahead of their feet as they move.

Dribbling

Players must dribble (constantly bounce) the ball as they run down the court. They often place their body between the ball and their opponents to protect it. A dribble often ends in a pass or a shot.

Netball

Starting as women's basketball, netball developed into a separate sport played by all. Quick passes and teamwork win netball. From set zones on the court, players must pass the ball to team members without bouncing it before shooting it into a netted hoop in the opposition's goal area.

PLAYERS Two teams of seven players each

DURATION 60 minutes (four 15-minute quarters)

PLAYED ON Wooden indoor court or grassy or asphalt outdoor court, 100 ft (30.5 m) long and 50 ft (15.2 m) wide

Volleyball

A player stretches to hit the ball from below and stop it from touching the ground.

Two teams take turns to serve a ball over a high net and try to score points by hitting the ball so the opposing team cannot return it. The receiving team has up to three touches of the ball to propel it back over the net and into their opponent's half of the court.

PLAYERS Two teams of six players each

DURATION Until one team wins three sets

PLAYED ON Wooden indoor court or grassy outdoor court, 60 ft (18 m) long and 29.5 ft (9 m) wide

Beach volleyball

Although similar to volleyball in rules, this variant of the sport is played on a smaller sand court with a smaller ball. It demands quick reactions and spectacular dives to keep the ball in play, especially in typically windy conditions. Players must move rapidly on the sand, smashing the ball over the net to the opposition and forcing them into missing hits.

PLAYERS Two teams of two players each

DURATION Until one team wins two sets

PLAYED ON Sand court, 52.5 ft (16 m) long and 26 ft (8 m) wide

The ball is made of waterproof materials and weighs about 9–10 oz (260–280 g).

A 28 ft (8.5 m) long net divides the court into two equal halves.

Italian players at a 2015 beach volleyball tournament in Ostia, Italy

FOCUS ON...
SHOTS

Attackers can use different shots to send the puck toward the goal at speeds as high as 120 mph (190 kph).

▶ The puck is driven powerfully with a full swing of the stick in a slap shot.

▲ The puck is pushed away quickly with the flick of a wrist in a wrist shot.

◀ The puck is struck unpredictably with the back of the blade in a backhand shot.

Ice hockey

Known simply as hockey in the US and Canada, this action-packed sport is played on an ice rink between two teams on skates. Players use wooden sticks to battle for control of a rubber disc called a puck, which they must shoot at their opponent's goal to score goals (points). In North America, the largest professional ice hockey league is the National Hockey League (NHL).

PLAYERS Two teams of six players each

DURATION 60 minutes (three 20-minute periods)

PLAYED ON Ice rink, 200 ft (61 m) long (no fixed width)

Ivan Muranov (in red) of Russia scores a goal past goaltender Cayden Primeau and player Phil Kemp (both in white) of the US at a 2019 game in Vancouver, Canada.

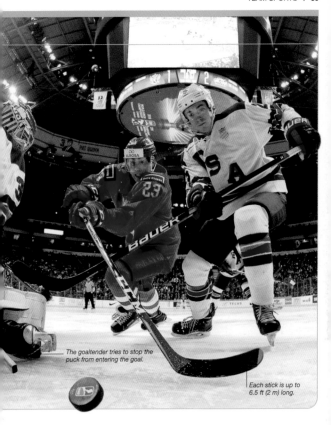

The goaltender tries to stop the puck from entering the goal.

Each stick is up to 6.5 ft (2 m) long.

Field hockey

In this team sport, two teams pass and dribble a hard ball around a long pitch using the flat end of their sticks. They aim to score goals past defenders and a heavily padded opposing goalkeeper.

PLAYERS   Two teams of 11 players each

DURATION   70 minutes (two 35-minute halves)

PLAYED ON   Rectangular grass or artificial pitch, 300 ft (91.4 m) long and 180 ft (55 m) wide

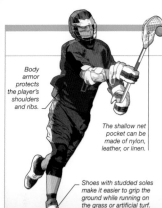

Lacrosse

One of the fastest-growing sports in the US is lacrosse. Moving at a quick pace, two teams try to score goals by using a cross—a stick with a netted pocket—to dribble and scoop up a hard ball, carry it, and then fling it with force into the opposing team's goal.

Body armor protects the player's shoulders and ribs.

The shallow net pocket can be made of nylon, leather, or linen.

Shoes with studded soles make it easier to grip the ground while running on the grass or artificial turf.

PLAYERS Two teams of 10 players each (men) or 12 players each (women)

DURATION 60 minutes (four 15-minute quarters)

PLAYED ON Rectangular field, up to 300 ft (110 m) long and 180 ft (55 m) wide

Tug of war

Two teams pull on a long rope in opposite directions. The team that "tugs" the other team toward a center line or a certain length of distance wins that round.

PLAYERS Two teams of eight players each

GEAR 115 ft (35 m) long rope, boots with flush soles and heels

JUDGED ON Best of three pulls

Jai alai

A player serves a ball against the front wall of a three-walled court. They score a point if the other player fails to return the ball before it touches the ground twice.

PLAYERS Two teams of one or two players each

GEAR *Cesta* (basketlike wicker racket), *pelota* (ball), helmet, elbow pads

PLAYED ON Three-walled court, 176 ft (53 m) long and 50 ft (15 m) wide

Racket sports

Players use rackets to reach farther and strike the ball or shuttlecock with a variety of shots—some involving full power and others a delicate touch. In many racket sports, players can add spin to the ball to send it curving through the air, making it harder for their opponent to return it.

STRETCH FOR SUCCESS
Swiss tennis legend Roger Federer lunges to reach the ball at the French Open. This sport demands an ability to stretch and recover with agility.

Racket sports

All racket sports demand agility, hand-eye coordination, and quick reactions. Matches are played between two players (singles) or two pairs of players (doubles), who hit a projectile back and forth, trying to score points with precise shots.

Tennis

Players strike a ball over the net toward their opponent and aim to prevent them from returning the ball. Players try to score points to win games and sets.

PLAYERS One or two on each side

GEAR Tennis racket, tennis ball

PLAYED ON Rectangular court, 78 ft (23.77 m) long and up to 36 ft (11 m) wide

Japanese tennis star Naomi Osaka hits a shot at the 2021 Australian Open.

Table tennis

The paddle, made of wood, has a rubber surface.

Players strike a lightweight ball with dazzling speed and spin over a 6 in (15.25 cm) high net in this fast-paced clash. The opponent must return the ball before it bounces twice. Multiple games are played, each to 11 points.

PLAYERS One or two on each side

GEAR Paddle, table tennis ball

PLAYED ON Rectangular table, 9 ft (2.74 m) long and 5 ft (1.5 m) wide

FOCUS ON...
PROJECTILES

Beating an opponent in a racket sport depends on striking a projectile using different angles and strengths of shot.

▲ A table tennis ball is hollow and made of plastic.

▲ A badminton shuttlecock's 16 feathers fit on its skirt.

▲ A tennis ball is made of rubber and covered in felt.

Badminton

Unlike most racket sports that are played with a ball, badminton players hit a feathery shuttlecock over a high net, aiming for it to land in their opponent's half of the court.

PLAYERS One or two on each side

GEAR Badminton racket, shuttlecock

PLAYED ON Rectangular court, 44 ft (13.4 m) long and 20 ft (6.1 m) wide

Real tennis

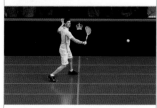

Most popular in the 16th and 17th centuries, this sport was the original form of tennis. It is played on indoor courts surrounded by four irregularly shaped walls, three of which have sloping roofs that shots can be played off.

PLAYERS One or two on each side

GEAR Real tennis racket, heavy cork ball

PLAYED ON Rectangular indoor court, typically 96 ft (29.3 m) long and 32 ft (9.8 m) wide

Tennis shots

A variety of shots can be played in tennis, often depending on the position of the player, their opponent, and the ball. To outwit their opponent, a player can vary the power, pace, and placement of each of these shots.

Groundstroke
A groundstroke is mostly played from the back of the court after the ball has bounced. The forehand and the backhand (above) are the main types of groundstrokes.

Volley
For this shot, the ball is struck before it has bounced by the player who is at or approaching the net. Volleys are often punched to direct the ball out of the opponent's reach.

Lob and smash
A lob sends the ball over the head of an opponent to land in the court behind them. A poorly executed lob might enable the opponent to play a powerful overhead smash in return to win the point.

A ball goes high in a lob shot.

Playing on a court

Games are played on a court marked by baselines, sidelines, and center lines. Each point of a game begins with an overhead shot, called a serve, taken from behind the baseline.

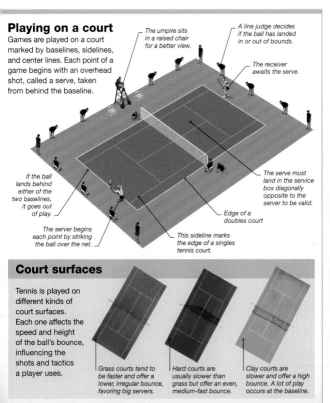

The umpire sits in a raised chair for a better view.

A line judge decides if the ball has landed in or out of bounds.

The receiver awaits the serve.

If the ball lands behind either of the two baselines, it goes out of play.

The serve must land in the service box diagonally opposite to the server to be valid.

The server begins each point by striking the ball over the net.

Edge of a doubles court

This sideline marks the edge of a singles tennis court.

Court surfaces

Tennis is played on different kinds of court surfaces. Each one affects the speed and height of the ball's bounce, influencing the shots and tactics a player uses.

Grass courts tend to be faster and offer a lower, irregular bounce, favoring big servers.

Hard courts are usually slower than grass but offer an even, medium-fast bounce.

Clay courts are slower and offer a high bounce. A lot of play occurs at the baseline.

Squash

In an enclosed court, players take turns hitting a ball against the front wall to score points, which they do when their opponent fails to return the ball before it has bounced twice. Players rally, trying to outfox their opponents and get them into positions where they cannot play the ball.

PLAYERS One or two per team

GEAR Squash racket, squash ball

PLAYED ON Rectangular court, 32 ft (9.75 m) long and 21 ft (6.4 m) wide

Colombian player Miguel Angel Rodriguez drives a powerful shot at the 2018 PSA Squash World Series.

The squashable rubbery ball used in this sport gives it the name squash.

Racquetball

Similar to squash but played using a longer racket and a bouncier ball, racquetball is a fast-paced sport that involves a lot of running. Like in squash, all four walls are in play as long as the ball strikes the front wall.

The racket is secured to the player's wrist with a strap.

PLAYERS One or two on each side

GEAR Wide-framed racket, safety goggles, rubber ball

PLAYED ON Rectangular court, 40 ft (12.19 m) long and 20 ft (6.1 m) wide

María José Vargas (left) of Argentina returns a shot to Paola Longoria (right) of Mexico in a 2019 match in Lima, Peru.

Pickleball

Players use paddles to serve a ball across a net in this fast-paced sport. Opponents must return the serve before the ball hits the ground twice.

PLAYERS One or two on each side

GEAR Paddle, plastic ball with holes

PLAYED ON Rectangular court, 44 ft (13 m) long and 20 ft (6.1 m) wide

Paddle tennis

Players serve the ball underhand across a net using paddles like in pickleball. The first to get four points wins a game, six games wins a set, and three sets wins a match.

PLAYERS Two on each side

GEAR Solid racket, rubber ball

PLAYED ON Rectangular court, 50 ft (15 m) long and 20 ft (6.1 m) wide

Combat sports

Head-to-head battles of technique, skill, strength, and bravery demand dedication in training and rapid reactions during a bout. Contests are frequently tense, exciting, and explosive. One mistake or moment of genius can determine the outcome of a competition.

POWER THROW
A judoka explodes into action, lifting and throwing their opponent during a European Championship bout in Bucharest, Romania.

Combat sports

Many combat practices developed out of ancient military training or systems of self-defence. Most combat sports today pit two competitors against each other in bouts overseen by judges.

Boxing

Fought over timed rounds, a boxer launches punches while trying to avoid their opponent's attacks. The punches are given points by judges. The aim is to outscore the opponent or knock them out so they cannot continue the bout.

DURATION 3–12 rounds of three minutes

HELD IN Boxing ring, up to 25 ft (7.3 m) on each side

JUDGED ON Landed punches, knockouts, one boxer unable to continue

Muhammad Ali (right) fights Trevor Berbick (left) in the Bahamas in 1981.

From 1928 to 1947, British boxer Len Wickwar fought a record 472 professional bouts.

Mixed martial arts

Fighters can strike, kick, throw, or wrestle their opponent in mixed martial arts (MMA), which uses techniques from other sports, such as boxing, muay Thai, and judo.

DURATION 3–5 rounds of five minutes

HELD IN MMA ring

JUDGED ON Knockouts, performance, submission (one fighter giving up)

Kickboxing

Moves from boxing combine with kicks from martial arts in this sport. Points are given for punches as well as high and low kicks. Similar rules for winning apply as in boxing.

DURATION 3–12 rounds of up to three minutes

HELD IN Boxing ring, up to 25 ft (7.3 m) on each side

JUDGED ON Punches, kicks, jumping kicks

Scholastic wrestling

Popular in US high schools and colleges, this style of wrestling takes place over three timed periods. Wrestlers are awarded points for holds above and below the waist as well as for control of their opponent's body position.

DURATION Three rounds of 2–3 minutes

HELD IN Wrestling mat, 39 ft (12 m) on each side

JUDGED ON Throwing and pinning an opponent to the mat under control

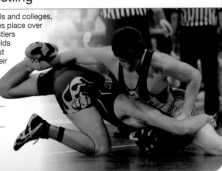

Sumo

Originally from China, this sport was popular only in Japan until the 20th century. It takes place on a raised platform called a *dohyo*, which is marked with a central ring. Wrestlers, some weighing more than 440 lb (200 kg), use timing and power to tackle their opponent.

DURATION Bout continues until a winner is determined.

HELD IN *Dohyo*, 18.8 ft (5.7 m) on each side

JUDGED ON Throwing the opponent off balance or out of the ring

A wrestler tries to make their opponent touch the ground with a part of their body other than their feet.

Japanese sumo wrestler Ōrora Satoshi weighed a record 645 lb (292.6 kg).

Aoiyama (left) grapples with Wakatakakage (right) at the 2021 Grand Sumo Spring Tournament in Tokyo, Japan.

Ju-jitsu

In one version of this sport, fighters called jutsuka display their balance and strength as they try to score points by striking and throwing their opponent to the ground.

DURATION Typically 2–10 minutes long

HELD IN Square competition area, up to 33 ft (10 m) on each side

JUDGED ON Technique and form in striking, throwing, and submission

Fencing

Players called fencers lunge, dodge, and defend themselves with blunt-tipped, swordlike weapons in this sport. The fencers are fitted with electronic sensors to register hits by their opponent's weapon.

DURATION Three bouts of three minutes

HELD IN *Piste*, a raised platform, 46 ft (14 m) long

JUDGED ON Touches of opponent's sword on target areas, the first to score 15 points

Judo

A close-range hand-to-hand combat sport that developed from ju-jitsu, judo involves sparring between two opponents called judoka. The pair grapple without punches or kicks—each trying to unbalance and throw their opponent or pin them down on the ground.

DURATION Five minutes (men), four minutes (women)

HELD IN Square competition area, up to 33 ft (10 m) on each side

JUDGED ON Technique, quality of throws and pins, first to gain an *ippon* (highest score)

Judo points

Bouts between judokas—supervised by two corner judges as well as scorers and timekeepers—begin with the shout of *Hajime!* ("beginning" in Japanese) by the referee, who awards points and issues warnings. The competitor with the most points wins.

Field of play

The competition area is made of padded mats called *tatami*. Most of the action occurs in the main contest area bordered by a danger zone, which is surrounded by a larger safety area.

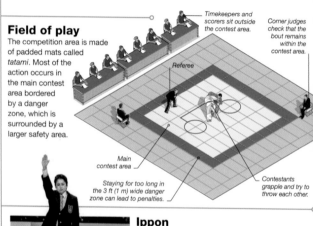

Timekeepers and scorers sit outside the contest area.

Corner judges check that the bout remains within the contest area.

Referee

Main contest area

Staying for too long in the 3 ft (1 m) wide danger zone can lead to penalties.

Contestants grapple and try to throw each other.

Ippon

When a referee awards an *ippon* (highest score), the bout is over in favor of the attacking judoka. Only a perfect throw landing an opponent on their back or a controlled hold for 20 seconds can gain an *ippon*.

Pinning holds

A judoka can use a number of moves designed to hold an opponent's shoulders squarely onto the mat. A controlled pin held for 10–19 seconds can earn a lesser point called a *waza-ari*. Two of these equal an *ippon*.

Throws

Judokas try to outwit and unbalance their opponents so they can throw them to the mat. Throws might involve launching an opponent over a shoulder or hip.

The hip acts as a pivot point when throwing an opponent in a hip throw.

A competitor can use their legs to sweep away one of their opponent's legs in a leg throw.

Submissions

An *ippon* can also be gained through a submission where one judoka forces their opponent to give up. This can occur as the result of a strong holding technique or arm locks called *kansetsu waza*.

Kung fu

Many different martial art styles from China are collectively known as kung fu. One style is *Sanda*, which is similar to kickboxing but includes wrestling and throws.

DURATION   Three rounds of two minutes

HELD ON   Raised platform

JUDGED ON
Clean strikes
to opponent,
knockouts

Karate

In sparring matches called *kumite*, karateka (karate fighters) fight each other in timed bouts to score points by striking, kicking, and throwing their opponent to the ground.

DURATION   2–3
minutes for *kumite*

HELD ON   Competition
area with padded
mat, 26 ft (8 m) on
each side

JUDGED ON
Clean kicks and
punches to
opponent's
target areas

Taekwondo

Competitors score points by using combinations of kicks and punches to an opponent's head, neck, or torso or by knocking them out in this explosive and popular martial art from Korea.

**Azerbaijan's Gashim Magomedov (left)
fights South Korea's Chan-Ho Jung (right)
at a 2016 match in Burnaby, Canada.**

DURATION Three rounds of two minutes

HELD ON Padded mat, 36 ft (11 m) on each side

JUDGED ON Kicks and hand strikes on opponent's target areas, knockouts

By 2021, Steven López (USA) was the only five-time winner at the World Taekwondo Championships.

Krav maga

Self-defense and getting in shape are the key elements of krav maga. Its methods include strikes, kicks, punches, and ground fighting as well as defenses against these techniques.

GEAR Body pads

HELD ON Mats in gyms

JUDGED ON Not judged (not a competitive sport; focused on defending oneself)

Muay Thai

Landing blows with fists, elbows, knees, and feet lets fighters gain points in the grueling bouts of this Thai martial art.

DURATION Five rounds of three minutes

HELD ON Square ring, 20–24 ft (6.1–7.3 m) on each side

JUDGED ON Clean strikes, knockouts

Water sports

Among the oldest of all modern sports are ones played in or on the water, including swimming and sailing. The action-packed races and events in water sports also feature divers hitting the water elegantly, surfers battling waves and currents, and rowers competing in ultimate tests of power and stamina.

WORKING TOGETHER
The swimmers of a Swiss synchronized swimming team perform in tandem with one another at a world championship in Spain.

Water sports

Sports played in or on the water—from swimming and diving to kayaking and surfing—are an exciting blend of speed, stamina, power, and grace. Competitions in water sports have featured at every modern Olympics since 1896.

Diving

After they jump from a platform or springboard, divers perform acrobatic moves containing twists and somersaults before plunging into a swimming or diving pool. Judges mark each dive for its moves and smoothness of entry into the water.

TYPE Solo or duo (synchronized)

GEAR Swimsuit

TOP EVENTS 1 m and 3 m springboard, 10 m platform

British diver Tom Daley competes in the men's 10 m platform final at the 2019 FINA Diving World Series in London, UK.

Swimming

Using one of the four main swimming strokes, swimmers race against one another over a set distance. Relay races pit teams of swimmers against each other.

TYPE Solo or team (up to four swimmers)

GEAR Swimsuit, swimming cap, goggles, ear plugs

TOP EVENTS Pool swimming individual (50–1,500 m), pool swimming relays, open-water swimming

FOCUS ON...
SWIMMING COURSES
Swimming competitions can be held in a swimming pool or in open water—in lakes, rivers, and seas.

▲ Indoor pools are 82 ft (25 m) in short course and 164 ft (50 m) in long course swimming.

▲ Open-water courses can cover 3 miles (5 km), 6.2 miles (10 km), or 15.5 miles (25 km).

Synchronized swimming

Complicated routines are performed in time to music by solo swimmers, pairs, or teams in this water sport, which was invented in Canada. The routines, which are marked by judges, feature movements that demonstrate the swimmers' strength, grace, and flexibility.

TYPE Solo or team (up to 10 swimmers)

GEAR Swimsuit, nose clips

TOP EVENTS Free and technical routines, 2.5–5 minutes long

Spain's women's national team performs in Mallorca, Spain.

SUPER SARAH

Sarah Sjöström of Sweden slices through the water in a 100 m freestyle competition at the 2017 FINA World Championships in Hungary. By 2021, she held more world records than any other female swimmer with six in total—in long-course freestyle (50 m and 100 m) and butterfly (50 m and 100 m) and in short-course freestyle (200 m) and butterfly (100 m).

It takes the best freestyle swimmers less than

one minute

to complete a 100 m swim

Swimming strokes

In the 19th century, swimming became a competitive sport, and over time, different styles or strokes of swimming developed. The four main strokes used by swimmers today are the front crawl, backstroke, breaststroke, and butterfly. Swimmers have to perform a single stroke in most individual races and all four strokes in medley races.

Starts and turns

Competitors jump off pedestals called starting blocks for the front crawl, breaststroke, and butterfly strokes, while backstroke swimmers begin their race already in the water. In most swimming races in pools, swimmers must make turns between each pool length.

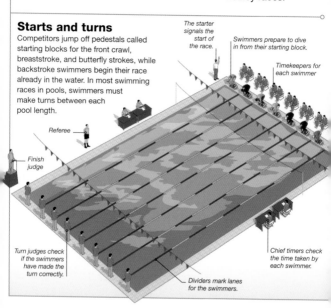

The starter signals the start of the race.

Swimmers prepare to dive in from their starting block.

Timekeepers for each swimmer

Referee

Finish judge

Turn judges check if the swimmers have made the turn correctly.

Chief timers check the time taken by each swimmer.

Dividers mark lanes for the swimmers.

Front crawl

The fastest of all strokes, the front crawl (also known as the freestyle) sees the swimmer's body roll from side to side as the legs kick alternately. Each arm enters the water ahead, then is drawn back powerfully.

Breaststroke

In this stroke, the arms stay in the water at all times, making a semicircular movement by pushing forward before pulling back to the swimmer's sides. This is followed by a kick and a short glide.

Backstroke

The backstroke is the only stroke that is swum faceup. Each stroke made through the water involves the arm traveling up and over the head, while the feet kick the water to maintain form. This stroke is also called the back crawl.

Butterfly

Good coordination is needed between the arms, legs, and body in the butterfly, which is the hardest stroke to perform. In it, the arms plunge into the water together ahead of the shoulders before they are pulled back powerfully. The feet kick together throughout this stroke.

Waterskiing

Pulled by a speeding motorboat on a lake or a river, a water-skier slices through water at great speed in this exciting sport. Competitions include ramp jumping for distance, trick routines for displaying spectacular stunts, and weaving between buoys in the quickest possible time in slalom events.

TYPE Solo

GEAR Water ski, towline, waterproof boots, life jacket, wetsuit, helmet (for some events)

TOP EVENTS Slalom, jumping, trick skiing

In 1922, at the age of 18, American Ralph Samuelson became the first person to water-ski.

US water-skier Blaze Grubbs competes in a men's slalom waterskiing event at the 2020 Moomba Masters in Melbourne, Australia.

The towline attached to a motorboat is kept stretched for the water-skier to maintain their speed.

Water polo

Often compared to a mix of swimming, volleyball, and rugby, this fast-moving ball sport is played by two teams in a pool—each trying to throw a ball into their opponent's goal. Players might swim up to 2 miles (3 km) during a match.

TYPE Team (seven players)

GEAR Water polo ball, swimsuit, swimming cap with ear guards

TOP EVENTS
Team competitions

Surfing

Riding towering ocean waves while standing on a lightweight surfboard takes balance, agility, and nerve. In competition, surfers are judged on their ride time on breaking waves and the slick moves they manage to perform.

TYPE Solo

GEAR Surfboard, wetsuit, safety leash

TOP EVENTS Longboarding, shortboard competitions, big wave events

Sailing

In competitions, sailing boats—which vary from small solo dinghies to giant ocean-racing yachts—are raced around set courses using just the wind to propel them forward. Events might be held on lakes, near the coastlines, or out on the biggest oceans.

TYPE Solo or team (up to 20 sailors)

GEAR Wetsuit or pants and waterproof jacket, boots, gloves, life jacket

TOP EVENTS Fleet racing, match racing, team racing

Rowing

Between one and eight rowers sit in narrow boats—each pulling one or two oars to propel their craft backward as quickly as possible.

TYPE Solo or team (up to eight rowers)

GEAR Oars, racing suit, goggles

TOP EVENTS Sprint races, head races

Kayaking

Kayakers control their kayaks with their whole body, propelling and steering their craft with a two-bladed paddle.

TYPE Solo or team (up to four kayakers)

GEAR Double-bladed paddle, waterproof top, foam-filled vest

TOP EVENTS
Flatwater sprint, slalom, kayak, polo, marathon

Canoeing

Flexibility and stamina are useful in the sport of canoeing. Canoeists typically kneel in their narrow canoe, propelling it with a single-bladed paddle. They compete in flatwater races on calm waters or timed slalom events on rapids.

TYPE Solo or team (up to four canoeists)

GEAR Single-bladed paddle, waterproof top, foam-filled vest

TOP EVENTS Canoe sprint (200–5,000 m), whitewater slalom

Rowing to win

Rowers propel their craft with power and pace. Rowing boats can range from single-person vessels to those capable of carrying nine people. Competitions usually involve a small number of craft racing to win in a straight line over a set distance on a calm flatwater course.

Types of rowing

There are two types of rowing, based on the number of oars used by rowers. Each rower uses two oars in sculling (left), while they grip one oar with both hands in sweeping (right).

The bow is the first rower over the finish line.

The six leads the four rowers in the middle.

The stroke sets the pace for the rest of the crew.

Equipment

Rowing boats are narrow and lightweight, made from carbon fiber and plastic. Rowers sit on a sliding seat with their shoes bolted to a footplate. Oar sizes can vary, with shorter oars used for sculling.

The tapered bow of the boat slices through the water.

The oar is a hollow carbon fiber tube with a flattened blade at the end.

Bowside rower

Strokeside rower

Rowing strokes

Each stroke consists of a powerful drive by the legs in coordination with the arms and body as the oar is powered forward through the water.

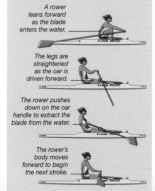

A rower leans forward as the blade enters the water.

The legs are straightened as the oar is driven forward.

The rower pushes down on the oar handle to extract the blade from the water.

The rower's body moves forward to begin the next stroke.

Rowing eight

Boats used for rowing can range from one that carries a single skuller to a 65.2 ft (19.9 m) long craft called an eight that can carry eight oarsmen and the coxswain (cox).

The cox steers the boat and calls the rate at which the oarsmen make strokes.

Kiteboarding

Using a handheld kite powered by the wind, kiteboarders are whisked along on their floating board in open waters at high speeds as they perform jumps and tricks.

TYPE Solo

GEAR Kite, board, wetsuit, life jacket

TOP EVENTS Course racing, freestyle, slalom, wave riding

Underwater sports

Modified versions of some sports, including soccer, hockey (below), and rugby are played underwater in pools with weighted balls or pucks.

TYPE Team (up to six players)

GEAR Swimsuit, flippers, mask, snorkel, swim cap

TOP EVENTS Underwater hockey, rugby, and soccer

Stand-up paddleboarding

With just a single-bladed paddle to power and steer themselves, paddleboarders compete in surfing and whitewater races against the clock.

TYPE Solo or team (up to nine paddlers)

GEAR Paddleboard, paddle, helmet, life jacket

TOP EVENTS Sprint races, distance races (5–35 km)

Windsurfing

Windsurfers can reach speeds over 50 mph (80 kph) as they angle their board's sail in and out of the wind. They race around courses marked with buoys or perform freestyle routines scored by judges.

TYPE Solo

GEAR Board, sail, wetsuit, waist harness

TOP EVENTS Speed sailing, wave jumping, freestyle, slalom racing

The sail catches the wind to help propel the board across the water.

German windsurfer Klaas Voget

Wakeboarding

Competing one at a time, participants are towed behind boats and use their boat's wake to perform aerial stunts. Judges score their performances based on the difficulty and execution of their stunts.

TYPE Solo

GEAR Wakeboard, helmet, boat, rope

TOP EVENTS Standard, free ride, cable, wake skate

The rider steers using the handle at the end of the rope behind the boat.

Personal watercraft (PWC) racing

Riders use their powerful watercraft in high-speed races or to perform stunts in freestyle events. Races usually include up to 10 competitors who ride craft that can move faster than 60 mph (100 kph).

TYPE Solo

GEAR PWC, helmet, goggles, life jacket, back protector, racing boots

TOP EVENTS Closed circuit speed races, offshore speed races, freestyle

Winter sports

Whether flying over a snow-covered ski slope or performing intricate moves on ice, elite athletes make winter sports look easy. Most of these sports require great core and leg strength, coordination, and balance to race or perform while staying in control on the most slippery of surfaces.

SPEEDY SLIDER
At the mercy of nature and yet in control, a skeleton rider hurtles down a track headfirst during a competition in St. Moritz, Switzerland.

FOCUS ON...
EQUIPMENT

Competitors in winter sports take care in preparing their skis and snowboards. They also use protective gear and goggles.

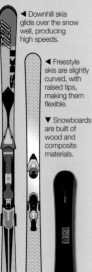

◀ Downhill skis glide over the snow well, producing high speeds.

◀ Freestyle skis are slightly curved, with raised tips, making them flexible.

▼ Snowboards are built of wood and composite materials.

Winter sports

Originating from unique ways to travel over snow and ice, winter sports have developed into exciting racing events and freestyle competitions.

Snowboarding

Using a ski-like board, snowboarders compete in races down mountain slopes, through a course with jumps and turns, and around gates (flags). They also perform routines of tricks and moves, marked by judges, on large U-shaped ramps called half-pipes or over ramps and rails in slopestyle competitions.

TYPE Solo or team

GEAR Snowboard, boots, helmet, padded pants, goggles, wrist protectors

TOP EVENTS Slalom, giant slalom, snowboard cross, half-pipe, slopestyle, freestyle

Skiing

In this sport, also known as alpine skiing, competitors ski down sloping, snow-covered courses marked out with gates as they race against the clock. Events include downhill, with a focus on speed; slalom, with closely spaced gates and many twists and turns; and giant slalom, with turns but not as many direction changes as slalom.

The helmet protects the skier from impacts.

Tight-fitting clothes enable greater speeds.

TYPE Solo

GEAR Skis, ski poles with hand straps, bodysuit, helmet, goggles, ski boots

TOP EVENTS Downhill, slalom, giant slalom, super giant slalom

German skier Marina Wallner

Freestyle skiing

Instead of racing against the clock or each other, skiers perform routines of jumps and tricks marked by judges for technical merit, accuracy, and style. Aerial slope courses feature high ramps to jump from, while mogul courses are covered in moguls (small snow bumps).

Ski poles are used by the skier to turn and propel themselves forward.

TYPE Solo

GEAR Skis, ski poles, helmet, goggles, ski boots

TOP EVENTS Moguls, aerial, acroski (ski ballet)

Freestyle skiers can reach heights of 40–50 ft (13–15.2 m) when jumping off ramps.

Skiing downhill

Downhill skiers race as short and fast a line down a course as possible. Maintaining good form and switching between turns, jumps, and the tucked position ensures maximum speed, which can often exceed 74.5 mph (120 kph).

Fast start

A run begins with the skier surging through a starting gate, which triggers the electronic timing. The skier pushes hard with ski poles to drive forward.

Racing tuck

When traveling in a straight line, racers adopt a tucked position, which makes their bodies as streamlined as possible to reduce air resistance. They hold their ski poles close to their sides, parallel to the ground, with hands in front, knees bent, and skis riding flat and parallel.

The ski poles are light and strong, with a comfortable grip.

Modern skiing developed in the Norwegian mountains in the 1800s.

Turning

Skiers shift their body weight and angle to stay low through turns and not lose time. They often make carving turns on the edge of their skis.

Jumping

During the multiple jumps on a downhill ski course, skiers fly through the air in a crouched position. They land in the tucked position to lose as little speed as possible.

SPEEDING THROUGH THE SNOW
Skiers compete in a ski cross race at the 2021 FIS Freestyle World Ski Championship in Idre, Sweden. Ski cross is a form of skiing. Four skiers compete at average speeds of 40 mph (64 kph) to cross the finish line in races held on challenging courses—up to 3,900 ft (1,200 m) long—full of bumps, turns, and jumps.

The skiers in a ski cross race spend

25 percent

of their race time flying through the air

Ski jumping

Starting at the top of a steep sloping ramp, jumpers crouch over their long skis as they speed down it before taking off. They hold their body position to fly over the greatest distance through the air before landing safely. Competitors are judged on their distance and style.

TYPE Solo or team (up to four jumpers)

GEAR Skis, safety helmet, goggles, jumpsuit

TOP EVENTS Normal hill, big hill, team big hill

The skier wears a jumpsuit made from a thin artificial fabric, which reduces air resistance.

Jumpers often hold their skis in a "V" shape during flight to increase air lift, which helps them fly over a greater distance.

Luge

Lying on their back on a narrow fiberglass sled, lugers race feetfirst down an icy course. They can reach terrifying speeds of up to 87 mph (140 kph) and steer by small movements of their shoulders and legs. The athlete with the quickest time wins in luge and skeleton.

TYPE Solo or duo

GEAR Bodysuit, helmet and visor, streamlined shoes with smooth soles

TOP EVENTS Timed multiple runs

Bulgarian luger Pavel Angelov competes at the 2014–15 Luge World Cup in Altenberg, Germany.

The sharp metal runners are called steels.

Bobsledding

In this fast winter sport, after pushing their sled during a sprint start, a team of two or four jumps inside a capsule-like sled, which hurtles down a twisting, icy course against the clock. The driver steers, picking the fastest possible way to complete the run.

TYPE Team (two or four riders)

GEAR Helmet, racing suit, shoes with spikes

TOP EVENTS Two-person bobsled, four-person bobsled

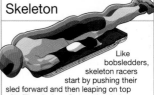

A tapered nose reduces air resistance, which makes the sled move faster.

The name "bobsled" comes from early racers who bobbed back and forth inside their sleds to increase speed.

The brakeman gets in last and controls the sled's speed.

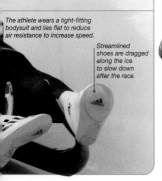

The athlete wears a tight-fitting bodysuit and lies flat to reduce air resistance to increase speed.

Streamlined shoes are dragged along the ice to slow down after the race.

Skeleton

Like bobsledders, skeleton racers start by pushing their sled forward and then leaping on top of it. They lie face-first on the sled as they hurtle down a frozen twisting track, which is at least 1,300 yd (1,200 m) long.

TYPE Solo

GEAR Speed suit, helmet and visor, cleated shoes

TOP EVENTS Timed multiple runs

Ice dancing

Balance, coordination, and grace are tested in this type of figure skating performed on an ice rink. Pairs of skaters are judged on three artistic routines choreographed to music. The pair cannot perform jumps and only certain types of lifts or holds are allowed. So they must express their skating and dance skills through footwork and body movements.

TYPE	Duo
GEAR	Skating boots, tailored costumes
TOP EVENTS	Rhythm dance, free dance

Spanish ice dancers Sara Hurtado (right) and Kirill Khaliavin (left) compete at the 2021 World Figure Skating Championships in Stockholm, Sweden.

Each pair of skates is specially designed for the skater.

Figure skating

Skaters perform turns, spins, and jumps on the ice over two routines to impress the judges. They are marked for style and technical accuracy.

TYPE Solo or duo

GEAR Skating boots, tailored costumes

TOP EVENTS Short, free skate

Speed skating

In long-track events, speed skaters compete in pairs, moving in lanes, against the clock. In short-track events, up to six competitors try to cross the finish line first.

TYPE Solo or team (up to three skaters)

GEAR Skating boots, hooded bodysuit

TOP EVENTS Individual (500 m–10 km), team pursuit, relay

Czech speed skater
Martina Sáblíková

Biathlon

Combining skiing and shooting, biathletes race on courses that are 6 miles (10 km) or longer. They stop up to four times to shoot rifles at targets and they receive time penalties for misses.

TYPE Solo or team relay (up to four skiers)

GEAR Skis, ski poles, rifle, bodysuit

TOP EVENTS Individual, sprint, relay, pursuit

Telemarking

Telemark skis are shorter and more maneuverable than traditional skis. Races involve elements of alpine skiing, Nordic skiing, and ski jumping. The aim is to complete the course in the quickest time.

TYPE Solo

GEAR Telemark skis, ski poles, ski boots, helmet

TOP EVENTS Classic, sprint classic, parallel sprint

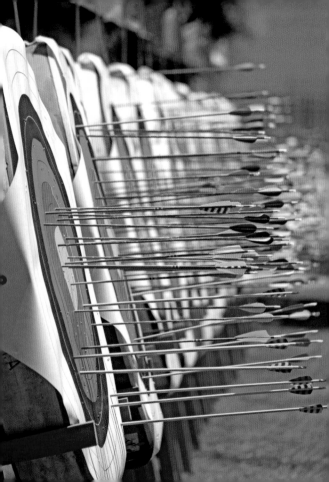

Target sports

From hitting a hole in golf to striking a target with an arrow in archery, target sports are all about aiming and executing each shot or move perfectly—and with unerring accuracy. Competitors need an excellent eye, a steady hand, and the ability to stay calm and in control at all times.

SNOOKER SHOT
Australia's Neil Robertson lines up his shot, aiming to pot the black ball into a pocket and leaving the white cue ball perfectly positioned for his next shot.

FOCUS ON...
GOLF CLUBS
Golfers carry up to 14 clubs in their bag—each capable of propelling the ball different distances and on different flight paths.

◀ A driver is a large-headed club used to strike the ball long distances.

◀ A mid-iron has an angled blade to send the ball forward and upward.

◀ Putters are used on the green or short grass near it to roll a ball into a target hole. This shot is called a putt.

Target sports

Hitting the target is the name of the game in these sports, which demand pinpoint accuracy and the ability to repeat movements with precision time after time.

Golf

A lot of skill and practice helps golfers strike a ball with a club toward a distant target hole in as few shots (or strokes) as possible. A hole also refers to each section of the course from the tee box to the green.

TYPE Solo or team (up to 12 players)

GEAR Golf clubs, golf ball, tee, spiked golf shoes, gloves

PLAYED ON Golf course, around 7,000 yd (6,400 m) long

In 1971, American astronaut Alan Shepard became the only person to hit a golf ball on the Moon.

Australian golfer Hannah Green

Curling

Teams of curlers try to slide heavy circular stones along an ice rink with the aim to land them in the center of a ringed target area called the house to score points.

TYPE	Team (four curlers)
GEAR	Granite stones, broom, gloves
PLAYED ON	Ice rink, 146 ft (44.5 m) long and 14.5 ft (4.42 m) wide

Ten-pin bowling

Bowlers roll a heavy ball down a lane, aiming to knock over 10 bottle-shaped pins arranged in a triangle. Points are given for every pin knocked over.

TYPE	Solo or team (3–5 bowlers)
GEAR	Bowling ball, pins
PLAYED IN	Bowling lane, 60 ft (18 m) long and 3.4 ft (1.05 m) wide

Disc golf

Played with similar rules as golf, disc golf features a small flying disc that is thrown into a chained basket to complete each hole of the course. The aim is to play each hole in as few shots as possible.

TYPE	Solo
GEAR	Discs, target basket
PLAYED ON	Disc golf course, more than 6,000 ft (1,800 m) long

US disc golfer Shannon Winfield (right)

Playing golf

A game of golf is played over 9 or 18 holes. A golfer must play a variety of shots to complete each hole of a course. They must pick the right clubs and shots to land the ball in each target hole in as few shots as possible.

On the hole

Each hole starts at the tee box and ends on a green with a small target hole into which the ball must be sunk. From the first shot, golfers aim at the green or the fairway, which is the corridor of short grass between the tee and the green. Accurate shots help avoid hazards, such as streams, tall grass, and sand bunkers, that can trap the ball.

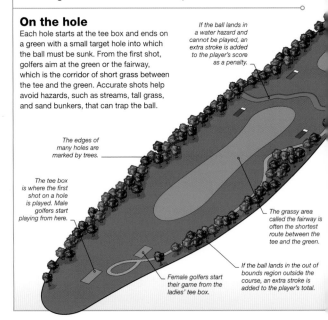

If the ball lands in a water hazard and cannot be played, an extra stroke is added to the player's score as a penalty.

The edges of many holes are marked by trees.

The tee box is where the first shot on a hole is played. Male golfers start playing from here.

The grassy area called the fairway is often the shortest route between the tee and the green.

If the ball lands in the out of bounds region outside the course, an extra stroke is added to the player's total.

Female golfers start their game from the ladies' tee box.

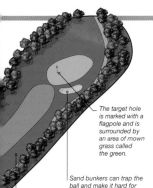

The target hole is marked with a flagpole and is surrounded by an area of mown grass called the green.

Sand bunkers can trap the ball and make it hard for it to be played from here.

Longer grass, called the rough, lines most fairways and can make the next shot harder.

On the green

A green is the closely mown grass surrounding a small target hole. A golfer must judge the slopes on the green and the speed of their stroke so their putt sends the ball into the hole.

The club cannot touch the sand before it touches the ball.

Sand traps

A common hazard across fairways and especially around greens is a sand bunker, or sand trap, which is a depression in the ground filled with sand. Golfers usually swing a heavily angled club to try to hit the ball out of the trap.

Archery

A rodlike stabilizer, which projects forward, helps to balance the bow vertically.

In archery competitions, archers use a bow to shoot up to 36 arrows in a round at a target made of different colored circles. Higher points are given the closer the arrow hits to the center of the target.

TYPE Solo or team (three archers)

GEAR Bow, arrows, quiver, arm guard, leather finger tabs

PLAYED ON Range, 295.25 ft (90 m) to the farthest target

Snooker

Players use a wooden cue to strike a white cue ball and pot (knock) the colored balls into the table's six pockets to score points.

TYPE Solo

GEAR Cue, chalk, white cue ball, 15 red balls, six colored balls

PLAYED ON Snooker table, 11.7 ft (3.57 m) long and 5.8 ft (1.78 m) wide

Pool

In this sport, players pot balls either in ascending number order (1–9) or pot all the striped or solid-colored balls.

TYPE Solo or team

GEAR Pool cue, chalk, white cue ball, 15 numbered balls

PLAYED ON Pool table, up to 8.2 ft (2.5 m) long and 4.3 ft (1.3 m) wide

Darts

A game of darts is a test of hand-eye coordination. Two players take turns throwing three darts at a dartboard. Each player starts with a score of 501 and their points are subtracted based on where the dart hits the board. The first player to reach zero in the fewest throws wins.

TYPE Solo

GEAR Three darts, dartboard

PLAYED ON Oche (elevated surface from behind which the dart is thrown), 7.78 ft (2.37 m) from the dartboard

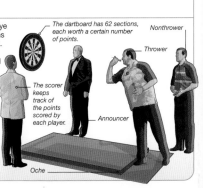

The dartboard has 62 sections, each worth a certain number of points.

Nonthrower

Thrower

The scorer keeps track of the points scored by each player.

Announcer

Oche

Billiards

Players score points by hitting their cue ball into the other cue ball and the red ball in one shot, using their cue ball to hit the red ball into a pocket, or hitting their cue ball into a pocket after hitting a red ball.

TYPE Solo

GEAR Cue stick, white ball, yellow ball, red ball

PLAYED ON Billiards table, 12 ft (3.7 m) long and 6 ft (1.8 m) wide

Croquet

Using mallets, players take turns hitting balls through nine hoops on the ground. The first player to hit the balls through all the hoops wins.

TYPE Duo or team (four or six players)

GEAR Croquet mallet, balls, hoops

PLAYED ON Croquet court, 105 ft (32 m) long and 84 ft (25.6 m) wide

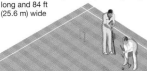

Wheel and motor sports

Fast—and sometimes furious—competitions involving quick-moving machines thrill spectators and challenge the fearless riders and drivers who need to make split-second decisions while racing against each other or against time. Not as fast-paced but just as exciting are some wheeled sports that let competitors perform dazzling tricks and moves.

PEDAL POWER
German cyclist Marcel Sieberg powers round a corner during a race at the Tour de Neuss, Germany. Bicycle races test a rider's stamina.

FOCUS ON...
BIKE TYPES

The designs of bicycles change based on the sport, but all take advantage of light and strong materials, such as carbon fiber, to reduce weight.

▲ A lightweight track bike has a single fixed gear and no brakes.

▲ A road bike is fitted with electronic gears and drop handlebars.

▲ A mountain bike has good suspension to cushion bumps.

Wheel sports

Sports on wheels began with chariot racing about 2,800 years ago. Modern-day wheel sports are action-packed tests of speed and feature a variety of racing events.

Track cycling

Track cyclists require great pace, acceleration, and tactical skills. They race around a banked oval-shaped track, measuring 273 yd (250 m) in Olympic competitions. Track races might feature sprint events, which pit two riders against each other, as well as longer endurance events.

TYPE	Solo or team (up to four cyclists)
GEAR	Track bike, streamlined helmet, track mitts
TOP EVENTS	Individual sprint, team sprint, team pursuit, Keirin, Omnium, Madison

Road racing

Hill climbs, long-distance stages, and sprints make road racing a tough test of a cyclist's fitness and stamina. The famous Tour de France features 21 days of road racing mainly across France.

TYPE Solo or team (up to eight cyclists)

GEAR Road racing bike, crash helmet, fingerless gloves, cycling shorts, team jersey

TOP EVENTS Time trials, criteriums, classics, multistage races

Mountain biking

Special bicycles are used in mountain biking. In cross-country races, bikers start at the same time and try to complete laps of a challenging hilly course with a finish line. In downhill competitions, riders race on steep courses against the clock.

TYPE Solo or team (up to six cyclists)

GEAR Mountain bike, gloves, body armor, helmet

TOP EVENTS Downhill, cross-country, four cross, endure, free ride

Thick, bumpy tires provide extra grip on loose ground.

Roller skating

Skaters perform trick routines on courses or take part in jump competitions. Many enter speed skating races on indoor or outdoor oval tracks, where they can reach speeds of more than 40 mph (64 kph). Depending on the event, skaters can choose between inline skates (with wheels in a row) and quad skates (with wheels in pairs).

TYPE Solo or team (up to 15 players)

GEAR Roller skates, streamlined helmet, wrist guards, kneepads, close-fitting jersey and shorts

TOP EVENTS Figures, freestyle, free dance, speed skating, vert skating

German skater Simon Albrecht leads during a men's speed skating 500 m quarterfinal at the 2017 World Games in Wroclaw, Poland.

A sharp angle lets a skater maintain their speed when going around a bend.

Roller hockey

Teams of players skate while passing a puck or ball around with long bladed sticks, aiming to score a goal by hitting it into their opponent's net. This fast-moving sport has many forms.

TYPE Team (five players)

GEAR Wooden sticks, roller skates, padded gloves, shin guards, kneepads, helmet

TOP EVENTS Rink hockey, inline hockey

Skateboarding

In this fast-paced sport, skateboarders pull tricks riding on and flying above ramps and U-shaped half-pipes in vert competitions or perform grinds over rails and ramps in street competitions. They also perform routines of tricks on the flat in freestyle events. Competitors are judged on their acrobatic skills, balance, and control of the board.

TYPE Solo

GEAR Skateboard, helmet, kneepads, elbow pads, gloves

TOP EVENTS Half-pipe, street, big air, vert

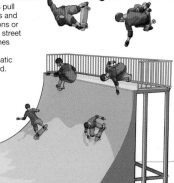

Motor sports

Ever since the first motor vehicles were developed, they have been pitted against each other in tests of speed, performance, and endurance. Today, a wide range of vehicles—from tiny karts to full-sized trucks—are raced.

Formula 1 racing

In this highly competitive motor sport, which has a formula (set) of rules to be followed, drivers race against one another in high-performance single-seat vehicles, scoring points depending on where they finish. Formula 1 cars compete at Grand Prix races—each held over multiple laps of a different twisting, turning race circuit. The driver and team with the most points at the end of a Formula 1 season are declared champions.

TYPE Solo (drivers belong to teams)

GEAR Formula 1 car, full racing suit, helmet, gloves

TOP EVENTS Formula 1 races

In the 2016 Mexican Grand Prix, Finnish driver Valtteri Bottas hit a record-setting speed of 231.4 mph (372.5 kph).

British racer Lewis Hamilton (left) goes neck and neck with Dutch racer Max Verstappen (right) in the 2021 Emilia Romagna Grand Prix race in Imola, Italy.

FOCUS ON...
RACE FLAGS

Flags are waved by Formula 1 race marshals to communicate warnings or actions to drivers as they speed by.

▲ A hazard has passed or been cleared and normal racing can proceed.

▲ The practice session, qualifying session, or race has ended.

▲ A faster car is behind a driver, who should let the vehicle pass.

Indy car racing

Open-wheel cars (with wheels outside the vehicle's main body) are used in Indy car races, which feature flying starts with vehicles already on the move, unlike in Formula 1. Drivers overtake each other to be the first to complete a set number of laps, scoring points based on where they finish. Top points for a driver or a team in a season means a championship victory.

TYPE Solo (no fixed number of drivers in a team)

GEAR Indy car, fire-resistant racing suit, helmet, head restraint, gloves

TOP EVENTS IndyCar® races

Karting

Karts are lightweight, small-wheeled vehicles raced mostly on scaled-down circuits. Different classes of competition are held, based on age groups and car performance.

TYPE Solo

GEAR Kart, helmet, visor, neck restraint, rib protector, racing suit, gloves

TOP EVENTS Sprint karting, endurance karting, speedway karting

Indy car racing

Drivers speed along oval or road racetracks, aiming to cross the finish line first, in this popular action-packed American sport. Although all Indy cars have the same chassis (basic skeleton) and high-powered engines, changes to the car, driver skill, and team strategy can be the difference between victory and defeat.

Speedsters

Indy cars are single-person seaters with an open cockpit. The chassis is made of strong carbon fiber and measures about 17.3 ft (5.12 m) long and up to 6.4 ft (1.95 m) wide, with a weight of at least 1,655 lb (751 kg). Different front and rear wings are fitted onto the chassis for different racetracks.

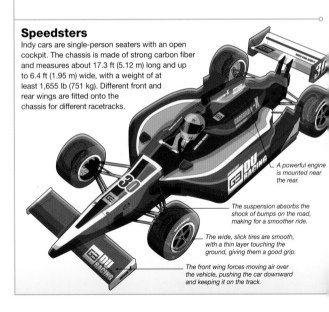

A powerful engine is mounted near the rear.

The suspension absorbs the shock of bumps on the road, making for a smoother ride.

The wide, slick tires are smooth, with a thin layer touching the ground, giving them a good grip.

The front wing forces moving air over the vehicle, pushing the car downward and keeping it on the track.

Large fuel tubes are used by fuelers to refill the tank.

Pit stops

During a race, a car can leave the track and enter a pit, where a six-person pit crew checks the vehicle. The crew can replace tires, perform repairs, make adjustments to the car's wings, and refuel the tank in less than 10 seconds.

The wheels are raised using an airjack for changing tires.

The tire changers can replace all tires in eight seconds or less.

Indy 500

Indy car racing gets its name from the Indianapolis 500 race, which features 200 laps of the historic Indianapolis Motor Speedway in Indiana, USA—a distance of about 500 miles (800 km).

FOCUS ON...
RACING TRACKS

NASCAR races are held on circuits of different lengths.

▲ The Daytona circuit is a 2.5 mile (4.02 km) long superspeedway.

▲ The Phoenix Raceway is a 1 mile (1.6 km) long circuit.

▲ At only 0.6 mile (858 m) long, the Bristol Motor Speedway is a short track.

NASCAR

NASCAR (National Association for Stock Car Auto Racing) races feature 43 drivers competing against each other in stock cars fitted with powerful engines. These hurtle around oval circuits at speeds in excess of 186 mph (300 kph). Cars bump and push each other in races that are frequently close and intense, with many lead changes that thrill fans.

TYPE	Solo
GEAR	Stock car, fire-resistant racing suit, helmet, racing gloves, thin-soled shoes
TOP EVENTS	NASCAR races

Jimmie Johnson won the 2011 Aaron's 499 NASCAR race by 0.002 seconds.

Stock cars race at Bristol Motor Speedway in Tennessee, USA, during the 2015 NASCAR Sprint Cup Series.

Portuguese driver José Rodrigues (right) races ahead of Germany's Fabio Citignola (left) at the 2019 European Truck Racing Championship in Misano Adriatico, Italy.

Motorcycle racing

Thrilling races for different types of motorbikes are based on engine capacity and held over laps on track circuits, roads, and off-road courses. Riders need balance, skill, and courage in these races, with some of them hitting speeds of more than 200 mph (320 kph). Safety is very important in motorcycle races.

TYPE Solo

GEAR Motorbike, padded racing suit, knee sliders, gloves, full-face helmet

TOP EVENTS motoGP, superbike, time trials, endurance, speedway

Truck racing

Big rigs speeding around a track at speeds up to 100 mph (160 kph) provide an eye-catching spectacle. Many races begin with a rolling start and are held over a set number of laps. Despite the vehicles' bulk, truck racing can be close and exciting.

TYPE Solo

GEAR Truck, helmet, seat harness, racing suit

TOP EVENTS Track racing, rally raids, truck rallycross, truck trials

Each truck weighs at least 6 tons.

Drag racing

Pairs of powerful cars called dragsters line up at one end of a straight drag strip to race. Such is their explosive acceleration that a 0.24 mile (400 m) race can take less than four seconds.

TYPE Solo

GEAR Dragster, fire-resistant gloves, racing suit, helmet, harness, head restraint

TOP EVENTS Top fuel, funny car, pro stock, comp, stock

The 2021 Dakar Rally was a grueling

4,774 mile

(7,683 km) long cross-country endurance race for motorcycles, cars, and trucks

Air racing

Pilots fly their aircraft around a fixed course, often marked by slalom-style air gates (pylons), in the fastest possible time.

TYPE Solo

GEAR Aircraft, pressurized flying suit, parachute, helmet, life jacket

TOP EVENTS Pylon races, cross-country

Snowmobiling

Powerboat racing

The world's fastest watersport features sleek boats skimming across open water at speeds of more than 155 mph (250 kph). Races are held from point to point or around a course marked by floating buoys.

TYPE Solo or team (crew of two)

GEAR Boat, helmet, seat belt, life jacket

TOP EVENTS Inshore racing, offshore racing, drag racing, match racing

Lightweight powerful snowmobiles are raced across tough terrain or on challenging snow-covered oval tracks with bumps and tight turns. A top-class snowmobile can go as fast as 120 mph (190 kph).

Motocross racing

Off-road motorcycles race for a set amount of laps around a curvy, jump-filled course. Races called supercross are held in stadiums.

TYPE Solo

GEAR Off-road motorbike, helmet, goggles, body armour, knee and elbow pads

TOP EVENTS Motocross, supercross, arenacross, freestyle motocross

24 Hours of Daytona

Over 24 hours, sports cars continuously race, swapping through 3–5 drivers, with the winner having run the most miles.

TYPE Team (five solo drivers)

GEAR Sports car, racing suit, helmet

HELD ON Daytona International Speedway, Florida, USA

US snowmobile racer Logan Christian (left) leads during a snowmobile snocross event at the 2016 Winter X Games in Colorado, USA.

TYPE Solo

GEAR Snowmobile, crash helmet and visor, racing boots, padded gloves

TOP EVENTS Cross-country racing, snocross, oval lap racing, hill climbing

Other sports

Some groups of sports stand on their own. These include competitions involving horses as well as regional sports, which are most popular in certain parts of the world. In recent times, these have been joined by exciting extreme sports that offer adrenaline-fueled action on land, in the air, and on and under water.

IN SYNC
Horses and their riders are in perfect harmony as South African polo players compete in a match against Chile.

FOCUS ON...
GROOMING

Competition horses are cleaned and groomed meticulously to keep them healthy and to make them look their best.

▲ A horse's thick coat is clipped to keep the animal cool.

▲ Brushing the coat removes dirt and mud and cleans the animal's skin.

▲ The horse's hooves are trimmed and debris is removed from them.

Other sports

Sports that test the speed, agility, or control of a horse and its rider are among the oldest of all. In contrast are new, high-risk extreme sports, which aim to thrill.

Polo

One of the oldest team sports in the world, polo might have been played for the first time more than 2,500 years ago. In this sport, riders from two teams use a long wooden mallet to strike a small hard ball, aiming to drive it into the opposing team's goal.

TYPE Team (four riders)

GEAR Mallet, plastic ball, polo saddle, kneepads, helmet, gloves

HELD ON Rectangular field, up to 300 yd (274.3 m) long and 200 yd (182.9 m) wide

Show jumping

A horse and its rider are timed as they complete a complex course with a variety of jumps over barriers. Knocking any over results in penalties.

TYPE Solo or team (up to four riders)

GEAR Riding helmet, jumping saddle, pants, jacket, riding boots with spurs

HELD ON Showjumping arena (no fixed size)

Dressage

A test of the training of a horse and its relationship with its rider, the sport of dressage features precise, choreographed movements performed by the horse under the close eye of a judging panel.

TYPE Solo or team (up to four riders)

GEAR Pants, jacket, riding boots

HELD ON Dressage arena, up to 197 ft (60 m) long

Horse racing

Millions of people gather at race courses around the world to enjoy horse racing's exciting contests of speed and endurance. These are held on flat tracks or over jump courses with hurdles that the horse and the rider, called a jockey, must clear.

TYPE Solo

GEAR Racing saddle, crash cap, goggles, racing silks, breastplate, pants, riding boots

HELD ON Flat race courses, steeplechase race courses (no fixed size)

2018 White Turf racing event in St. Moritz, Switzerland

Hang gliding

With nothing but air currents to propel them after jumping off a cliff or mountainside, competitors on hang gliders fly in aerobatic events or soar cross-country in speed and distance competitions. Each pilot lies suspended in a harness beneath their glider's triangular wing, which they turn by moving a control bar using shifts in their body position.

TYPE Solo

GEAR Glider, harness, sturdy shoes, helmet, visor, GPS receiver

TOP EVENTS Cross-country, accuracy spot landing, race to goal, open distance

The rigid wing works like an airplane's wing and is lifted by air.

Paragliding

The control of a winglike parachute called the paragliding wing enables paragliders to catch air currents and soar through the air, sometimes for hours, as they compete in aerobatics and cross-country racing.

TYPE Solo

GEAR Parachute, harness, seat, helmet, gloves, GPS receiver

TOP EVENTS Cross-country racing, accuracy spot landing

The pilot uses the control lines to steer the parachute.

Cliff diving

Strong nerves are needed to dive off a cliff and perform acrobatic moves before hitting the water. Judges mark the competitors, who are trained and take all necessary safety precautions.

TYPE Solo

GEAR Swimsuit

JUDGED ON Take off, acrobatics, entry into the water

Skydiving

Leaping from an aircraft and plummeting toward the ground while performing acrobatic moves is not for the faint-hearted. Skydivers jump from heights of up to 13,000 ft (4,000 m) and can reach speeds of 120 mph (190 kph) in a free fall before opening their parachutes to land safely. Events involve landing on a ground target and formations in the air by teams of skydivers.

TYPE Solo or team (4–16 skydivers)

GEAR Parachute, jumpsuit, helmet, goggles, harness, altimeter

TOP EVENTS Formation skydiving, vertical formation skydiving, free-form skydiving, canopy piloting

The US skydiving team in formation at a 2006 championship in Gera, Germany

Climbing

Sport climbing competitions are usually held on indoor walls or icy outdoor faces. Some climbers rely solely on their shoes and chalk on their hands for grip.

TYPE Solo or team (up to three climbers)

GEAR Shoes, helmet, ropes, crampons, carabiners, chalk

TOP EVENTS Lead climbing, speed climbing, bouldering

Whitewater rafting

Rafters use oars or paddles to control their inflatable raft as it hurtles downriver through churning whitewater rapids. Races are head-to-head sprints or timed runs down slalom courses.

Parkour

Lightweight shoes offer a good grip on brick, concrete, and steel surfaces.

Competitors require balance, strength, and agility in the sport of parkour. Using acrobatics, which include vaults, leaps, climbs, jumps, and rolls, they move freely and continuously on and around obstacles in a city, such as railings, walls, and steps.

TYPE Solo or team (up to 15 athletes)

GEAR Running shoes, loose clothes

TOP EVENTS Alive after 5, best trick, style, speed, pairs speed, dueling speed, relay

OTHER SPORTS | 141

TYPE Team (up to 12 paddlers)

GEAR Inflatable raft or dingy, collapsible paddle, oar, helmet, wetsuit, life jacket

TOP EVENTS Sprint, slalom, downriver

Free diving

Without using any breathing gear, free divers dive to the greatest depths possible in open water or cover as much distance as they can in a pool on one breath.

TYPE Solo or team (up to two divers)

GEAR Wetsuit, dive computer, weights and weight belt, nose clips, fins (in some events)

TOP EVENTS Dynamic apnea, static apnea

Free-ride mountain biking

Riders use a specially designed bike to complete a downhill course full of dirt jumps and ramps, getting airborne and performing exciting moves and tricks as they go.

TYPE Solo

GEAR Mountain bike, gloves, helmet, padded body armor

TOP EVENTS Big mountain, slopestyle, streetstyle

Dodgeball

Players from two teams throw balls at each other. A player is "out" when a ball hits them before hitting any other surface. The first team to get all the other team's players "out" wins.

TYPE Team (six players)

GEAR Foam or rubber balls

PLAYED ON Court, 50 ft (15 m) long and 25 ft (7.6 m) wide

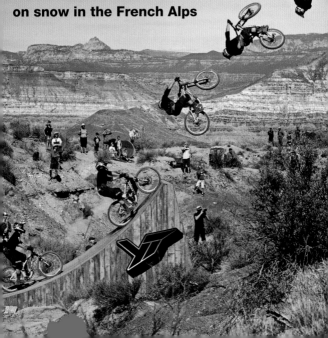

In 2017, extreme mountain biker
Eric Barone of France hit a record-setting

141.5 mph

(227.7 kph) while riding downhill
on snow in the French Alps

REMARKABLE RYAN
US mountain biker Ryan Howard flies off a wooden ramp in this time-lapse photo as he performs a spectacular backward somersault during the 2015 Red Bull Rampage competition in Utah, USA. Free-ride mountain biking mixes the acrobatic with the technical, using all of nature as a bike park.

Regional sports

Some sports are well known in one part of the world, where they sprung up and grew popular. Over time as people moved around the world, they brought with them the rules and equipment of their sports to share with new audiences. Many of these sports are celebrated in regional competitions.

Horse relay race

This indigenous American sport features a three-lap relay race on horseback, with each rider racing three horses around a track. A rider completes a lap on one horse before mounting a second horse and then a third. The action is fast and intense, as up to eight riders jump off one horse and mount another in this exciting and often chaotic sport.

TYPE Team (one rider, one mugger to grab the horse, two horse holders)

GEAR Reins

HELD ON Open ground or racecourse

A rider competes in the 2019 Blackfoot First Nations race in Alberta, Canada.

The competitors in a horse relay race ride bareback—none of the horses have a saddle.

Kabaddi

In this sport from India, two teams take turns to raid their opponent's half of the court, sending a player to tag a member of the opposing team. The raiding player has to hold their breath as they repeat the word *kabaddi* when trying to do this while avoiding being tackled themselves by the other team.

TYPE Team (seven players)

GEAR Sports shoes

HELD ON Court with mat, up to 42.7 ft (13 m) long and 32.8 ft (10 m) wide

Iran's Sedigheh Jafari (in red) tries to escape Indian players at a match in Jakarta, Indonesia.

Dambe

A traditional sport of the Hausa people of Nigeria, dambe sees two fighters punch, kick, and wrestle. Each of the three rounds only ends when one fighter is knocked down or submits.

TYPE Solo

GEAR *Kara* (rope wrapped around an arm)

HELD ON Contest area on level ground

Pok-ta-pok

Juego de pelota maya, as it is called in Spanish, is a revived version of an ancient Mesoamerican ball sport. Players may only use their hips to move a ball down a court, keeping it in the air and shooting it through a hoop.

TYPE Team (five players)

GEAR Solid rubber ball

HELD ON I-shaped court, 328 ft (100 m) long and 98 ft (30 m) wide

All about sports

MILESTONE MOMENTS

- **c. 1400 BCE** The first known ball courts are built to play a Mesoamerican ball sport in Central America.

- **776 BCE** The ancient Olympics are held for the first time, in Olympia, Greece.

- **1682** A golf match between Scottish and English players in Leith, Scotland, is one of the first recorded international sports matches.

- **1877** The world's first official international tennis championship is launched at Wimbledon, UK.

- **1891** Canadian-American educator James Naismith invents basketball in Massachusetts, USA.

- **1896** The first modern Olympics are held, in Athens, Greece.

- **1903** The first Tour de France cycle race is held, covering a distance of 1,509 miles (2,428 km).

- **1904** The Fédération Internationale de Football Association (FIFA), the global organization in charge of football, is formed.

- **1908** The Fédération Internationale de Natation (the International Swimming Federation/FINA) is formed to manage competitions in many water sports.

- **1920** The American Professional Football Association is established. Two years later, it is renamed the National Football League (NFL).

- **1924** The first dedicated Winter Olympics competition is held in Chamonix, France.

- **1947** NASCAR is formed and runs its first race the following year.

- **1955** A competition for the elite football clubs of Europe, the European Cup, is founded.

- **1960** The first official Paralympics are held in Rome, Italy.

- **1967** The Super Bowl is organized by the National Football League (NFL) for the first time.

- **1975** The first Cricket World Cup is held in England.

- **1991** The first FIFA Women's World Cup is won by the US national women's soccer team.

- **2000** Sixteen new women's events are added to the Summer Olympics.

- **2016** Rio de Janeiro in Brazil hosts the first Olympic games held in South America.

- **2021** The Tokyo Olympics are held after a year of postponement because of the COVID-19 pandemic.

Uruguay became the first country to win the FIFA World Cup in 1930.

ASSOCIATIONS, LEAGUES, AND CLUBS

- Formed in 1894, the **International Olympic Committee (IOC)** picks hosts for the Olympics and governs which sports are included at the games.

- The **National Basketball Association (NBA)** is the world's most famous basketball league, with 30 teams.

- Millions of Americans watch the annual Super Bowl – the championship game of the **National Football League (NFL)** season.

- Founded in 1992, the **UEFA Champions League** rebranding of the European Cup for top European football clubs is now club football's biggest competition.

- The most successful club in Major League Baseball (MLB), the **New York Yankees** had won 27 World Series championships by 2021.

- Founded in 1960, the American football team **Dallas Cowboys** had won five NFL Super Bowls by 2021 and was the first NFL team to be valued at more than US$4 billion.

- Founded in 1878 as Newton Heath LYR Football Club, **Manchester United**, English football's most successful team, changed its name in 1902 and moved to its Old Trafford stadium in 1910.

Quidditch, a fictional game in *Harry Potter*, is now a real-life sport in which players run with a broomstick between their legs.

UNIQUE SPORTS FROM AROUND THE WORLD

- The Scottish sport of **caber tossing** sees competitors toss a 16–20 ft (4.9–6.1 m) tall wooden pole (the caber) as far as possible.

- The traditional First Australian sport of **gorri** involves one player rolling a large disc of tree bark while others attempt to hit it.

- In **cycle-ball** (radball), a combination of cycling and football, teams of two players each use their bikes to shoot the ball at their opponent's goal.

- Argentina's national sport **pato** is played on horseback. In it, teams battle to grab a six-handled ball and throw it into a circular net.

- Launched in 2020, **Ultimate Tennis Showdown** is a new form of tennis with timed matches divided into four quarters. It was set up with the aim to make tennis more fast-paced.

- The Irish sport of **camogie** features two teams of 15 female players who use a curved wooden stick to lift and move a ball called a sliotar around a rectangular pitch.

- A traditional pastime of Ethiopia, **genna** is a hockey-like sport played with a wooden ball on a rectangular pitch.

- **Bossaball** is a volleyball-like sport that uses trampolines and gymnastics skills to spectacular effect.

Setting records

OLYMPICS AND PARALYMPICS

Most golds in an Olympic games
US swimmer Michael Phelps won a record eight gold medals at the 2008 Beijing Olympic Games.

Most Olympic appearances
Canadian show jumper Ian Millar appeared in 10 Olympic games, from 1972 to 2012.

Youngest Olympic gold medalist
Marjorie Gestring, from the US, was just 13 years and 268 days old when she won the 3 m springboard diving competition at the 1936 Olympics.

First to win Summer and Winter medals
US athlete Eddie Eagan won a gold in boxing at the 1920 Olympics and then a bobsled gold at the 1932 Winter Olympics.

Oldest Olympic medalist
Oscar Swahn from Sweden was 72 years and 280 days old when he won a silver medal for shooting at the 1920 Olympics.

Oldest female Olympian
The UK's Lorna Johnstone, who took part in dressage at the 1972 Olympics, was 70 years and 5 days old.

Most successful Olympian at the 2020 Olympics
US swimmer Caeleb Dressel won five gold medals at the 2020 Olympics, the most of any athlete at those games.

Most Summer Olympic medals (nation)
The US leads the way with 1,061 gold, 836 silver, and 738 bronze medals.

Best Olympic record of an Asian nation
Including the 2020 Olympics, Japan has won 169 gold, 150 silver, and 178 bronze medals.

Most successful Winter Olympic nation
Norway has topped the medal table at eight Winter games and has 368 medals.

Most Paralympic medals
US swimmer Trischa Zorn won 41 gold, 9 silver, and 5 bronze medals in her career.

Youngest Paralympian
Polish table tennis player Natalia Partyka was just 11 years old when she competed at the 2000 Paralympics, in Australia.

Most nations competing at a Paralympics
More than 4,300 athletes from 164 nations competed at the London Games in 2012.

Most Paralympic medals in different sports (at a single event)
Italian paraathlete Maria Scutti won 15 medals—10 golds, 3 silvers, and 2 bronzes—in shot put, javelin, club throw, table tennis, fencing, and swimming— all at the 1960 Paralympics.

Most Winter Paralympic medals
Ragnhild Myklebust of Norway won a total of 27 Paralympic medals, in ice sledge skiing, biathlon, and cross-country skiing.

OTHER RECORDS

Longest race winning streak
US track and field star Edwin Moses won 122 consecutive 400 m hurdles races between 1977 and 1987.

Most world track and field records set
Ukrainian pole vaulter Sergey Bubka set 17 outdoor and 18 indoor world records in his career.

Quickest multiple world records
In 1935, Jesse Owens broke three world records in track and field and tied with another—all in just 45 minutes of competition.

Most consecutive appearances
Cal Ripken Jr. played 2,632 games in a row for the Baltimore Orioles baseball team between 1982 and 1998.

Most NBA championship wins
Following the Los Angeles Lakers' victory in 2020, they are tied with the Boston Celtics for the most NBA championship wins, with 17 each.

NHL points record
Canadian Wayne Gretzky retired with 2,857 points in the National Hockey League (NHL).

Youngest Formula 1 winner
Belgian-Dutch driver Max Verstappen became the youngest Formula 1 driver to win a race with his victory in 2016 at 18 years and 228 days old.

German tennis legend Steffi Graf held the world no. 1 position for a record total of 377 weeks.

STRANGE BUT TRUE

• Ethiopian athlete Abebe Bikila won the marathon at the Rome Olympic Games in 1960 **running in bare feet**.

• In 2008, the Slovakian women's ice hockey team beat Bulgaria, 82–0, **scoring a goal every 44 seconds** on average.

• Australian Henry Pearce was so dominant in the 1928 Olympics single sculls rowing event, he stopped to **let a line of ducks pass** before continuing rowing to win a gold medal.

• At the 2020 Santander Triathlon held in Spain, **Spanish triathlete Diego Mentriga slowed down to let British triathlete James Treagle pass him and win**. Treagle had been leading but had taken a wrong turn about 328 ft (100 m) from the finishing line.

• The combined Danish and Swedish tug-of-war team at the 1900 Games was **an athlete short and asked Edgar Aaybe, a Danish journalist, to join in**. They went on to win the gold medal.

• In a 2005 English football match, referee Andy Wain lost his temper with the players. Once he calmed down, he **sent himself off for bad behavior**!

• Canadian skier Diana Gordon Lennox skied downhill in the 1936 Olympics with **one arm in a plaster cast**.

Glossary

Accelerate To increase one's speed.

Aerobatics Such stunts as tight turns, twists, and loop-the-loops performed in the air by aircraft.

Apparatus The equipment used by gymnasts to perform their routines on.

Athlete A general term for a person who takes part in a sport.

Attacker A player or a team that tries to score or help score points in a team sport.

Banked Something that is sloped or inclined.

Bout A match between opponents in many combat sports.

Buoys Floating markers that shape the outline of a course or turn in some water sports.

Carbon fiber A material containing many thin fibers of carbon that give it great strength but keep it lightweight.

Choreography The arranging of a series of movements in routines in some sports, such as figure skating.

Circuit A track on which races are held.

Cue A long pole of wood that snooker and pool players use to strike balls.

Cue ball A white ball that snooker and pool players hit using a cue before it strikes other balls on the table.

Diamond The area formed by the four bases on a softball or baseball field.

Dismounting The act of leaving a piece of gymnastics apparatus and landing safely on two feet.

Dribble To move a ball with multiple taps of the feet or bounces with the hand.

Freefall In skydiving, the action of falling through the air before the parachute opens.

Gates In skiing, the poles planted in the snow that define the route a skier must take down the course.

GPS Short for global positioning system. This electronic system helps people navigate and find out where they are.

Grapple To seize, hold, and wrestle with an opponent in some combat sports.

Half-pipe A U-shaped ramp used to perform tricks in such sports as skateboarding and snowboarding.

Hazard An obstacle, such as a sand trap or river, found on a golf course.

Home run A hit in baseball or softball that allows the batter to touch all four bases before being tagged out.

Ippon A winning point in judo, karate, and some other martial arts.

Knockout In combat sports, this is when a contestant knocks down their competitor so they cannot get up to finish the fight.

Lap A complete circuit of a running track or a racetrack in a wheeled or motor sport.

Martial art The name given to a number of sports that began as methods of self-defense or combat.

Olympics The biggest international sports competition, held once every four years. These are divided into summer and winter sports.

Opponent The person or team one competes against in a contest.

Paralympics The biggest international sports competition for many disabled athletes.

Penalty A punishment imposed on a player or team for breaking the rules of a sport.

Pitch To throw the ball to the person batting in softball or baseball.

Pit stop When a motor racing vehicle leaves a race and is attended to by its race team for refueling, repairs, or fitting new tires.

Professional An athlete who is paid to participate in a sport. Also refers to a type of sport in which athletes are paid to participate.

Projectile An object, such as a ball, shuttlecock, or dart, that is thrown into the air by a player.

Puck A rubber disc used to play ice hockey.

Rally An exchange of strokes or hits in a court game, such as tennis or volleyball, that ends when one team or player fails to make a good return.

Rebound In basketball, when the ball bounces off the backboard or hoop.

Referee An official usually in charge of a game or bout who ensures that the players follow the rules of the sport.

Relay A race in which each member of a team covers part of the total distance, known as a leg of the race.

Rink The ice on which skating sports, such as ice hockey and figure skating, are held.

Routine A series of movements in a sport.

Runway A long strip of track on which an athlete can build up speed before performing a vault or throw.

Serve In tennis, squash, volleyball, and some other sports, the action of striking the ball to begin play.

Slalom A type of race in which competitors must weave in and out of gates on their way to the finish line.

Smash A sudden powerful shot, usually struck overhead, in many racket sports.

Solo A single competitor in an event.

Somersault An acrobatic move in which a person turns head over heels in the air, starting and landing on their feet.

Special Olympics The biggest international competition for athletes with intellectual disabilities.

Spectators People who watch a sport—either live at the event or via TV or the internet.

Stamina The ability to compete for a long time.

Starting blocks Devices used by sprinters and swimmers at the start of a race.

Stock car Ordinary cars that have been upgraded for speed.

Submission In many combat sports, the act of one competitor giving up in a contest.

Substitute In team sports, a player who takes over from someone already playing because of an injury or a change of tactics.

Tackle To force a player to ground after grabbing them.

Tactics Methods of play used to outwit an opposition team.

Throwing circle A small, circular area from which an athlete must propel their discus, shot, or hammer in a track and field event.

Tie When the scores of two teams or two opponents are exactly the same.

Time trial A form of cycling competition in which cyclists are sent out at intervals to cover a specified distance on a road course in the quickest time possible.

Try A score in rugby league or rugby union, worth five points.

Wetsuit A close-fitting suit that keeps players warm when in water in events for water sports, such as sailing and open water swimming.

Whitewater rapids Parts of a fast-flowing river with a lot of churn in the water.

Index

Acknowledgments

Dorling Kindersley would like to thank the following people for their help with making the book: Sarah Macscoster for the Gymnastics section; Sreshtha Bhattacharya, Shatarupa Chaudhuri, Virien Chopra, Upamanyu Das, Arushi Mathur, Bipasha Roy, and Neha Samuel for editorial assistance; Balbhav Parida, Aparajita Sen, and Hena Sharma for design assistance; Vishal Bhatia for DTP assistance; Saloni Singh and Priyanka Sharma for the jacket; Caroline Stamps for proofreading; and Helen Peters for the index.

The publisher would like to thank the following for their kind permission to reproduce their photographs:

(Key: a-above; b-below/bottom; c-center; f-far; l-left; r-right; t-top)

123RF.com: Aleksey Satyrenko 87crb; **Alamy Stock Photo:** Action Plus Sports Images 40cla, Aflo Co. Ltd. / Nippon News 40bl, Agefotostock / Juan García Aunión 6cl, Ilyas Ayub 56tr, Simon Balson 5b, 16; Antony Baxter 43, Cal Sport Media / Jevone Moore 52bl, Cavan Images / Chico Sanchez 145crb, CPA Media Pte Ltd / Pictures From History 7cla, Am Cutting 108, Luke Durda 111cla, H. Mark Weidman Photography 94r, Christopher Hel 5cr, Gary Hill 137b, imageBROKER / Alessandra Sarti 137cra, imageBROKER / Daniel Schoenen 97cb, imageBROKER / Juergen Hasenkopf 63cb, ITAR-TASS News Agency / Andrew Chan 58-59, Andrew Lloyd 101tr, Guillem Lopez 25t, Malcolm Park editorial 66cla, mikecranephotography.com 2r, 98b, PA Images / Andrew Matthews 39tr, PA Images / Tony Marshall 24tr, Dusica Paripovic 5tl, Linda Richards 78cla, Rick Rudnicki 144, Jozsef Soos 132cla, Jon Sparks 119ca, Split Seconds 32, Split Seconds / Peter Llewellyn 78-79, Steven Scott Taylor 93cl, The Granger Collection 7b, UPI / Heinz Ruckemann 77tl, UPI / Jim Bryant 48bl, John Wellings 128tr, ZUMA Press / Mario Houben 34, Cavan Images 107br, Ken Howard Images 79br, Marcel Laponder 107bl, Stephen Vincent 95br; **Depositphotos Inc:** Igor_Vkv 3cra, 144cb; **Dreamstime.com:** Walter Arce 125t, 125br, 126cla, 126bl, 126-127, Asperiphoto 9cl, 52cla, Andrew Atkinson 67bc, Cristian Badescu 91b, Olga Besnard 107cla, Lukas Blazek 104-105b, 107cra, Blurf 83tr, 83b, Valentyn Burlachenko / Smilinghotei 138t, CarolRobert 109cb, Chelsdo 20cla, 73cla, 87clb, Elena Chepik 87tl, Chudtsankov 3ctb, Jerry Coli 48cla, Angelo Cordeschi 57, Aldo Di Bari Murga / Aldodi 50cb, Droopydogajna 128b, Fahrner78 121ca, Alexandr Finogentov 3ca, 88cla, Oliver Foerstner 67br, Vladimir Galkin 52clb, 75tr, Christos Georghiou 16t (x18 inside), Maciej Gillert 78bl, Ruslan Gilmanshin 6br, GoranJakus 99t, Ivan Hlobej 141bl, Cosmin Iftode 82br, Jborzicchi 90, Evren Kalinbacak 23br, Katatonia82 27tc, 27tr, Chan Yee Kee 65tc, Denis Kelly 46-47t, Kontakt883 117cb, Anna Kosolapova 136clb, Sergii Kumer 22, Manit Larpluechai 65bl, Chris Van Lennep 135cb, Agenzia LiveMedia 26bl, 128-129t, Marcogovel 140tl, Masuti 113cr, Matimix 9tr, MaxiSports 89ca, Miceking 3cla, 3cb, 21clb, 22crb, 99crb, 101tc, 105cra, Mogilevchik 3cb (golf), 110cb, Michele Morrone 95bl, Natursports 81cb, Lenar Nigmatullin 87tr, Ovydyborets 65tl, Photosvit 27tc (hoop), 29r, Pictac 50bl, Inara Prusakova 27cb, 29cla, Raywoo 17bl, Francois Roi 130-131, Pongphan Ruengchai 65tc (ball), Daniele Russo 136cla, Hafiza Samsuddin 3tr, 122crb, 127cra, Smallcreativeunit5 67bc (hardcourt), Akbar Solo 114tl, Stef22 71cb, 77b, StockPhotoAstur 123cr, Ljubisa Sujica 3tc, 72crb, 74cra, Tianothai 62, Ukrphoto 15cb, Viacheslav Vorobyev 35cb, Voyagerix 136bl, Weblogiq 104t, Maxim Yakup 132bl, Yobro10 3cl, 40cb, 47clb, 49cb, 52cb, Yurii Zushchyk 83tc; **Getty Images:** AFP / Bay Ismoyo 13t, 33t, AFP / Chaldeer Mahyuddin 145t, AFP / Daniel Leal-Olivas 65cr, AFP / Fabrice Coffrini 26r, AFP / Francois-Xavier Marit 84-85, AFP / Gerard Malie 40clb, AFP / Guillaume 40cb, AFP / Karim Sahib 68, AFP / Laurie Dieffembacq 13br, AFP / Oli Scarff 114bl, AFP / Philippe Lopez 118b, AFP / Pius Utomi Ekpei 145bl, AFP / William West 8B, Agence Zoom / Jonas Ericsson 102-103, Julio Aguilar 136b, Archive Photos / The Stanley Weston Archive 48clb, Naomi Baker 92-93b, Lars Baron 122b, Bongarts / Matthias Hangst 1, 73cra, 120, Clive Brunskill 66cra, Corbis Sport / VCG / Jerome Prevost 100-101, Denver Post / Andy Cross 101crb, Denver Post / Daniel Petty 132-133, David Finch 76bl, Focus On Sport 72b, Paul Gilham 20bl, Chris Graythen 126clb, Laurence Griffiths 28-29c, Matthias Hangst 21, Icon Sportswire / Brian Spurlock 123bl, Icon Sportswire / Michael Allio 129b, InsideFoto / LightRocket / Andrea Staccioli 8, International Skating Union / Joosep Martinson 106, Alika Jenner 36-37, 40-41, Matt King 42br, 64bl, Mark Kolbe 44-45, Kyodo News 30-31, MediaNews Group / Boulder Daily Camera 111b, MediaNews Group / Reading Eagle / Ben Hasty 73b, Daniel Milchev 142-143, Dean Mouhtaropoulos 60, National Basketball Association / Noren Trotman 54bl, NBAE / Andrew D. Bernstein 52-53, NCAA Photos / C. Morgan Engel 46-47b, NCAA Photos / Stephen Nowland 20cra, NurPhoto / Dominika Zarzycka 82bl, Mattia Ozbot 92cr, Doug Pensinger 10-11, PGA of America / Darren Carroll 110b, Stephen Pond 18-19, R&A / Matthew Lewis 113bl, Ezra Shaw 69t, Nathan Stirk 12br, Stone / David Madison 14, Scott Taetsch 39b, TASS / Sergei Bobylev 26bl, TASS / Sergei Fadeichev 96, The Asahi Shimbun 74, TPN 66br, Universal Images Group / Universal History Archive 7tr, Samo Vidic 141tc, Tim Warner 48-49, Andrew Wong 111cra, Anadolu Agency / Ali Atmaca 115bl, Boston Globe / Barry Chin 69br, Brian Cleary 133cr, NurPhoto / Artur Widak 33bl, Portland Press Herald / Ben McCanna 69bl, Patrick Smith 95cra; **Getty Images / iStock:** E+ / Aksonov 70, E+ / ihsanyildizli 134, E+ / shaunl 116; **Shutterstock.com:** AP 100clb, EPA / Joachim Priedemann 139, Evgeniyqw 80, evronphoto 140-141t, Volha Werasen 79cra

Cover images:

Front: **123RF.com:** luminis crb/ (helmet), radionphoto fcrb/ (Trampoline); **Dorling Kindersley:** W&H Golden Ltd / Dave King fbl; **Dreamstime.com:** Oleg Dudko cl, Konstantin32 cb, Stephen Noakes / Stevenoakes ca, Vudhikul Ocharoen cra, Denis Pepin fr, Phasinphoto fcr, Sergeycoh clb, Skypixel fbr, Zaclurs fclb, Zagorskid crb; **Fotolia:** Alex Mac cla; **Getty Images:** Corbis / Lew Roberston c; **Getty Images / iStock:** E+ / DNY59 fcrb/ (Pins), stuartbur fcrb, walik br, Weenee bc

Spine: **Getty Images:** Corbis / Lew Robertson

All other images © Dorling Kindersley. For further information see: www.dkimages.com

Other references

ncaa.org: National Collegiate Athletic Association. (2019). *Attendance Records.* (10tl)